Hope After Divorce

Hope After Divorce

Edited by Jennifer Cummings, Ph.D., Lisa LaBelle,

and Amy Osmond Cook, Ph.D.

Sourced Media Books, LLC

San Clemente, CA

Sourced Media Books, LLC
20 Via Cristobal
San Clemente, CA 92673
www.sourcedmediabooks.com

ISBN-13: 978–1–937458–20–1

Printed in the United States of America.

This publication is designed to provide information for inspirational purposes only and is sold with the understanding that the publisher is not engaged in rendering legal, accounting, or other professional advice of any kind. If legal advice or other expert assistance is required, the services of a competent professional person should be sought.

—From a Declaration of Principles jointly adopted by a
Committee of the American Bar Association and a
Committee of Publishers and Associations

Contents

Contents

Acknowledgments

First and foremost, we would like to thank our contributing authors, who have written such thoughtful, courageous, and faith-promoting essays. We thank you for sharing your powerful experiences and important messages. We are most grateful.

We would like to sincerely thank Virginia H. Pearce for writing the beautiful foreword. We would also like to thank Mandy Davis Clegg for her contributions to the book, as well as her efforts in sharing its important message with members of the community.

Thanks to our families for their unwavering support and love through this three-year collaboration.

Above all, we are grateful for our Savior, Jesus Christ. In Him, there is always hope.

Foreword

Virginia H. Pearce

"In one way or another, divorce touches most families. . . . We cannot control and we are not responsible for the choices of others, even when they impact us so painfully."[1] So spoke Elder Dallin H. Oaks in General Conference, April 2007. The prevalence of divorce seems to gain momentum with each passing decade. The reasons for it are legion. The individuals affected, impossible to count. The pain is overwhelming.

These are the individual stories of individual women. Their stories are theirs alone. But there is great commonality. Each is full of pain, and each has found relief and healing through the Atonement of Jesus Christ. Of a certainty, they will be encouraging to those who are experiencing the dissolution of their families. But these stories reach beyond the specificity of divorce and into every mortal experience that is pain-filled. They educate us. They soften us. They teach us. We find renewed hope in the Atonement of Jesus Christ. We are convinced, once again, that he offers healing balm and sustains us—no matter the wounds—if we will make the choice to turn to Him in our brokenness.

---

1. Oaks, D. H. (2007). Divorce. *Ensign,* May, p. 70.

On finishing the last page, the reader is filled with hope and gratitude for the goodness of God, He who gave each of His children agency, but then offered healing balm, even ordering all things for our good, as fast as we are able to receive them (D&C 111:11).

These women of faith can testify, along with Elder Oaks, "Whatever the outcome and no matter how difficult your experiences, you have the promise that you will not be denied the blessings of eternal family relationships if you love the Lord, keep His commandments, and just do the best you can."[2] When young Jacob "suffered afflictions and much sorrow" from the actions of other family members, Father Lehi assured him, "Thou knowest the greatness of God; and he shall consecrate thine afflictions for thy gain" (2 Nephi 2:1–2).

---

2. Oaks, D. H. (2007). Divorce. *Ensign,* May, p. 71.

Introduction

Jennifer Cummings, Ph.D., Lisa LaBelle, and
Amy Osmond Cook, Ph.D.

Divorce statistics paint a grim picture—something some of us have learned the hard way. Researchers project that fifty percent of first marriages will end in divorce over their lifetime, and second marriages fare even worse.[1] For people of faith, the outlook is somewhat brighter in that religiously committed people are less likely to divorce than non-religious people.[2] Still, there is reason for concern. As President Gordon B. Hinckley observed, "Divorce is much less frequent with those married in the temple. But even among these there is far more divorce than there should be."[3]

Divorce hurts everyone; and no matter how common it becomes in the world, nothing fully prepares one for a loss of this magnitude. Those who have walked, or are still walking, the fiery path of divorce can attest to the intense suffering that comes from broken hearts, broken dreams, and broken covenants. The devastation simply cannot be overstated. It can, however, be overcome.

In this collection of deeply personal narratives are the inspiring stories of ordinary LDS women and other Christian women of faith who, through their extraordinary faith and courage, have triumphed over the tests and trials of divorce. Each shares her personal sojourn through the labyrinth of divorce. Each is intimately acquainted with grief, anger, hurt, and fear. Between them, they have felt the wounds of abuse, the sting of betrayal, and the crushing blow of rejection. They have endured the kind of disappointment and despair that leaves one wondering whether anything in life can ever be made right again. They do not claim to have all the answers or to have done everything "right" in marriage or divorce—but they have walked through the refiner's fire and emerged with stronger faith. They are women who have relied upon the Atonement of Christ and have found hope and solace therein.

These women share their stories for the benefit of those who also find themselves in the dark and lonely hallways of divorce. Their message is one of good cheer with a promise of better days ahead. As each testifies, all things can indeed "work together for good to them that love God" (Romans 8:28).

Divorce is not the answer to all marital troubles, nor would it ever be our desire to encourage, promote, or glamorize the dissolution of marriage. For most of the women in this book, divorce was not a matter of choice but an undesired consequence of a spouse's decision to end a marriage. For others whose marriages turned abusive and degrading, divorce was the unfortunate consequence of what President James E. Faust called "a prolonged and apparently irredeemable relationship, which is destructive of a person's dignity as a human being."[4]

Ultimately, what leads to the breakdown of a marriage is complicated and cannot be attributed to one person or one gender; however, the question at the heart of this book is not how we get to the point of divorce but *how we get through it!*

By design, this book is about women's experiences with divorce—not because we see women as the sole victims of divorce, but because we know from experience the challenges of facing divorce as religiously devoted women. We have experienced personally the comfort that comes from knowing there are those who have walked the road before us and have survived and thrived.

While the authors hold in common their faith in Jesus Christ, they otherwise represent diverse backgrounds and circumstances. Some were married for decades, while others were married for months. Most had children at the time of divorce, but some did not. Some have since married again, while others have remained single. For a few, healing came quickly, while for others, wounds are still fresh. Some speak of the liberating power of forgiveness, while others make their way toward that goal one day at a time. Some have moved mountains to be able to stay at home with their children, while others have had new worlds of opportunity open up in their education and careers. Most express gratitude for family and friends who have walked with them through their darkest hours, and all testify of a Savior who succored them through their personal Gethsemanes.

The essays written by these admirable women offer us a glimpse of the shock, humiliation, and heartache that often comes with divorce; to gloss over this reality would be to obscure the gravity of such loss and minimize the devastation born of divorce. Notwithstanding, great care has been taken by the authors and editors of this book to ensure that their stories will not bring embarrassment to former spouses or family members. To that end, names and identifying circumstances in the narratives have been changed.

The resounding message we hope to convey is that through the Atonement of Christ, all can be made right. We *can* be made whole! Even in the bleakest of circumstances, faith, courage, hope, and reliance upon the Savior allow us to overcome any obstacle or disappointment, including divorce. We hope all who find themselves facing this or similar loss and heartache will be inspired by the testimonies of those who have tested the Lord's promise, "all flesh is in mine hands" (D&C 101:16), and have found it to be true.

We are never alone, and we have every reason to hope.

---

1. Wilcox, W. B., and Marquardt, E., Eds. (2011). The state of our unions: When marriage disappears, pp. 71–72. Poulsbo, WA: Broadway Publications.

2. Raley and Bumpass (2011). Topography of divorce. In Wilcox, W. B., and Marquardt, E., Eds. (2011). *The state of our unions: When marriage disappears,* pp. 71–72. Poulsbo, WA: Broadway Publications.

3. Hinckley, G. B. (2003). Loyalty. *Ensign,* May, p. 59.

4. Faust. J. E. (1991). Father, come home. *Ensign,* May, p. 36.

1

Hope and Life After Divorce

Alone in my bedroom, it wasn't the first time I had fasted and knelt in prayer in search for answers; but, I felt an urgency I had never felt before. As I pleaded on my knees, I was overcome with a sense of calm. Tears streamed down my face, and I knew what I needed to do. Nervousness and fear gave way to confidence in Him. I stood up and, while wiping away my tears, listened as Heavenly Father whispered, "You are doing the right thing. Have faith, and I will carry you every step of the way. Listen and stay true. Be kind. Pay your tithing. Don't carry anger. Just love."

The next day, I walked into the court room, secure in my decision. I stopped fighting over all the "stuff," which in the end would come to mean nothing, anyway. The torrent of doubt and sadness of the previous year finally came to an end. I walked away with renewed confidence in my new life with my beautiful one-year-old daughter, Olivia.

Aside from the frightening ordeal of court proceedings and starting over with a new life, I basked in a newfound confidence that surprised even my parents. How was I, a new mother with a young infant, going to support our little family? I had not worked since Olivia was born and had moved to a new city. What little money I had was going towards the attorney's fees. But I knew that Heavenly Father would sustain me, and I was immensely grateful for his love and mercy.

The first Sunday in my home ward after my divorce was challenging. Many of the sisters were so kind to Olivia and me, but others were less compassionate. I heard unkind whispers that hurt: my poverty, my health, my prospects, and my baby were all subjects of speculation and gossip for an unhappy few. Rather than lashing back or reacting, I resolved to never be judgmental or unkind to others going through trials. Those kind sisters who stood by me in the difficult times were angels to Olivia and me. How grateful I am for those compassionate souls.

I faced an uncertain future—one that, among other things, would be filled with awkward dates, unwanted match-making, and blended families. Still, I resolved to be open to life's possibilities.

After a difficult year, I went to Utah to spend time with my brother's family. While there, I was invited to attend a wedding reception with a friend. Being recently divorced, I found it difficult to look at the fresh, happy faces of newly married couples without being overwhelmed by emotions ranging from abject failure to hostility and jealously. But in sticking with my resolution to be open to the future, I accepted the invitation and went to the wedding.

As we arrived at this lovely reception, my friend left me to my own devices while he caught up with old friends. Not wanting to call the evening a total loss, I started up a great conversation with a pair of charming and very funny sisters who felt like old friends. We talked most of the evening; and as we parted ways, the younger sister mentioned she was going to be relocating to Southern California, close to where I was living. I hoped to meet her again and become friends.

A few months later, my bishop suggested that I attend the local singles ward. Then, he offered me some very valuable advice. He asked me to list the top ten most valuable traits that I desired in a future husband. It felt corny and a little bit like a Young Women's fireside activity, but I came home and made the list. I listened to my heart and the Holy Ghost. I thought about past relationships, good and bad, and was honest with myself about what really mattered. It stretched me, challenged me, and gave me a clear vision of what I wanted for my future.

I followed my bishop's advice and went to the singles' ward over the next few months. One day, close to Christmas, as I got ready to attend Sacrament Meeting, I felt peace and a bit of excitement. The future was uncertain but filled with possibilities. Not wanting to go alone, I invited my little sister to join me. More than ever, I felt that there was a plan, a purpose, and a very loving Father in Heaven who was directing my path. It was a wonderful Sacrament Meeting. After the meeting at the ward's Linger Longer, I ran into one of the very funny and charming sisters that I had met at the wedding reception in Salt Lake City. We struck up a conversation for a few minutes before her older brother arrived.

"Hi, I'm Ryan."

"Hey, I'm Andrea."

After introductions and the story about how his sister and I met, the flirting began in earnest. Unfortunately, in that acoustically challenged cultural hall, I didn't hear his name properly. So, when the bishop came around to meet the new faces, I introduced "Ryan" to the bishop as "Brian." As he corrected me with a smile, I blurted out, "Well, I guess that makes one less person that's going to ask me to that darn Christmas dance." To my surprise, he asked for my number and promised to call.

As a single mother, sometimes I preferred a night a home with Olivia, eating popcorn and watching a movie instead of going out. I simply didn't have the energy to keep up a social life. This was how I felt when Ryan called me four days later, asking me to join him to watch the local symphony play that evening.

The moment of truth came when I informed him very casually that I would have to find a babysitter for my two-year-old daughter and would call him back. I didn't particularly want to go out that night; so after a half-hearted attempt to find someone,

I called him back with a very polite excuse that I couldn't find anyone to help. Expecting a quick answer and a race to get off the phone, I was pleasantly surprised and caught off-guard when he answered, "That's ok by me. Why don't I come down, and we can all go out to get some ice cream at McDonald's?" Seeing he was not easily dissuaded, my parents offered to help, and we made plans for him to pick me up that night.

As I dropped off my daughter at my parents' home and waited for Ryan to arrive, I couldn't for the life of me remember what he looked like. I remembered a warm smile and a great laugh but not much else. When he arrived, he was more handsome than I remembered and nice enough not to give me a hard time with the terrible directions that I had given him. He was introduced to my parents and Olivia, and he warmly greeted both. In my experience, one of the first subjects on the first date is usually centered on my past—and this was no different. However, I learned very early not to answer with bitterness or sadness but with honesty and hope. I wouldn't spend time on the details and simply said, "I was married to someone, but we are both better off as good friends." This seemed to answer the question perfectly for Ryan, and the subject didn't come up again. As we talked, I became more attracted to him and interested in the things he had to say. I will admit that I let him do a lot of the talking. He was clever, and the conversation flowed naturally.

After the concert, I asked him more about his funny sisters. He told me all about his very large family and the fun they had together. Impressed at his answer, I asked more about his mom. I was inspired by a mother that could raise a family in the gospel that enjoyed life so much. For the first time that evening, he paused before he answered; and then he choked up as he explained that she had passed recently and that the family was struggling with her loss. Then, in seeing his sadness, I started to tear up. Together, we sat crying and laughing as he told me some funny and tender stories about his mom and family. It struck me at the time that if this man could love me and treat me with the same kind of respect that he showed for his mother, then we could have a wonderful life together.

During the drive home, we were chatting about something, and I felt an overwhelming feeling that this was the man that I would marry. Of course, not wanting to scare him away, I played it cool and begrudgingly accepted a second date. Since then, we have never been apart. Interestingly enough, after the first few dates, I pulled out the Top 10 list that the bishop told me to make. It matched up to about six out of ten qualities, which isn't too bad!

For me, life after divorce means that you have to go on living. You have to be open to possibilities, take risks, and hope for the best—even when faced with a constant stream of the mediocre. There is a path, one which our Heavenly Father knows well and will help us walk if we put our trust in Him and look forward to the future with hope.

2

Mission Impossible

I was 20 years old and decided that if I did not get engaged by 21, I would go on a mission, something I had always considered. On my 21st birthday, I got engaged and ended up, instead, going on "Mission Impossible." I had always sort of had my life planned out. I wanted to go to college at BYU, meet a wonderful guy, get married in the temple, have babies, be a stay-at-home mom, and live happily ever after. Well, I have learned that life rarely goes as planned.

Shortly after becoming engaged, I finished that semester at school and moved back home to plan for my upcoming wedding. My fiancé stayed back in Utah, his home, to work. While I was home in California, I had many doubts about the marriage but just assumed it was wedding jitters and the fact that we were apart. As the wedding date came closer, the doubts became more intense. I decided that if I did not feel "right" about this huge decision when we went through the temple together, three days before our wedding, then I would call it off. I explained this to my fiancé, and he agreed that we would pray first and then go to the temple together. He still wanted to get married but said it would be wise to call off the wedding if I did not feel it was the right decision.

I prayed all night Wednesday, then went to the temple Thursday morning for the first time. I had such a good feeling that this marriage was the right thing to do. So, that Saturday, I was married for time and all eternity in the Los Angeles temple.

In the beginning, I was so happy that I was on my way to fulfilling my dreams. But the dreams later turned into nightmares. Our marriage was not turning out as I had planned, and neither was my husband. He was not living up to the covenants he had made in the temple; and after three years, he decided he wasn't sure he wanted to be married, anymore. One night, he explained that he just wasn't sure about us. He got in his car and drove away. That was seventeen years ago, and I literally have not seen him since.

I was numb and in shock. In the days that followed, I felt as if I were living in someone else's body or having an out-of-body experience. I drove my car and looked at other people on the street, wondering how life could possibly still be going on around me. I went to the doctor's office to have my TB test read, so I could start a teaching job and realized that the people around me had no idea what I was going through. They had no idea! They could not feel my pain or know of my misery or the road ahead for me. They could not know that I felt as if I were dying inside or that I wanted to actually die.

I moved back home with my parents. As friends began to find out what had happened, they made many comments like, "He's an idiot!" and "Good thing you didn't have children." While I can appreciate the sentiments now, at the time telling me that my husband whom I loved and married was an idiot did not help. Nor did the fact that we did not have children. I kept thinking that if we had children, then maybe he would change his mind— or at least I would be able to see him again. I could not think of anything worse that could happen to me. Even if he had died and I had been left a widow, at least we would be together again. Even if one of us had a terrible disease, or no money, or no children, at least we would be together and still following Heavenly Father's plan.

The thought of divorce was unbearable to me. That was not something that happened to good Mormon girls, and it was definitely not part of His plan. How could I ever recover from this? This was never in my plans. Never once did I imagine my future including the word "divorce." But here I was, going through one.

I prayed and pleaded with Heavenly Father to make my husband change his mind and come back to me. I wanted to do anything I could to make things right. I was completely depressed and could barely live my life, let alone think straight. I would pray for help and then, in the same prayer, become so angry with my Father in Heaven that He would let this happen. I just could not understand. I knew I was not perfect, but I was trying to do everything right. How could something like this happen to me?

I would lay in bed sobbing; then I would think of ways to kill myself. I convinced myself that I would be okay, that I could stop thinking about it, because I would be dead the next day. Fortunately, I was busy with a new teaching job and too tired and smart to go through with anything that horrid.

Luckily, I had wonderful, loving parents and family and friends close by. My mom made me an appointment with my home ward bishop; very hesitantly, I went. I did not want to be told what to do and that it was my fault and I must have done something wrong. How inspired my bishop must have been, because everything he said was right and exactly what I needed to hear. He even told me I did not have to go back to church immediately, which I was dreading because of what people would think.

That same week, I participated in a market research study to make a little extra money. I was still not myself, and my mom had made me that appointment and had even driven me to the study. I sat next to a lady named Stacey, who was very talkative. I didn't feel like talking, but I listened. She finally told me, for some reason, that she lived next to the Mormon church—my ward building! She was, in fact, LDS but hadn't been to church for years because she had no one to go with. Even in my awful state of confusion about whether my Heavenly Father even listened to or loved me, I knew I could not let this opportunity pass by. I invited her to church with me that Sunday and told her I would meet her there. I could not believe I said that, but now I was committed. I went back to my family ward that Sunday, and guess who didn't make it? Stacey. I have never seen her again. But I knew that God works in mysterious ways, because I don't know how or when I would have gone back to church.

A good friend of my family took me back to the temple with my parents. He had also been divorced and was now happily remarried. He told me that I had two choices: to stay in the church through this and trust in the Lord, or to become frustrated and lose my faith and testimony. I decided to stay, even though this was a huge trial of my faith. At the time, I didn't know if I even believed, anymore.

I also received an amazing letter from a couple, Steve and Cindy, that have been longtime family friends. They both told me how wonderful I was and that bad things happen to good people. Steve even made me a list of qualities I needed to look for in my future husband. Along with looking for someone with a strong testimony who honors his priesthood, he also listed "good kisser." This was the first time I thought that maybe someday I would be healed enough to find someone else and truly be married for time and all eternity.

I met many incredible people after my divorce who had been through similar experiences and found that the scripture in D&C 122:7 applied to all of us:

> And if thou shouldst be cast into the pit, or into the hands of murderers, and the sentence of death passed upon thee; if thou be cast into the deep, if the billowing surge conspire against thee; if fierce winds become thine enemy; if the heavens gather blackness, and all the elements combine to hedge up the way; and above all, if the very jaws of hell shall gape open

the mouth wide after thee, know thou, my son, that all these things shall give thee experience, and shall be for thy good. (D&C 122:7)

My trials and tests of faith brought to me a greater understanding of the Lord's plan and helped me to gain a stronger testimony—a testimony that no matter what our problem, trial, or opposition in this life, Heavenly Father never leaves us. He always gives us a way to come back to Him and feel His love if we only let Him in. I also gained a greater understanding of others and the fact that we just never know what trials someone might be going through. Someone may feel like she is dying inside and may need the comfort of another person in a smile, a friendly hello, or a reassurance that she is loved. Looking back now, I can see that my divorce helped me to become a better person and to trust in the Lord. I knew that Jesus suffered and felt every pain and emotion that we have; and finally realizing that someone else felt my pain and knew exactly what I was going through helped me to know that everything would be okay.

I began going to the singles ward in our stake on the one condition that my cousin, who had been inactive for a few years, would come with me. I figured it was just as hard for him to go as it was for me. We ended up helping each other through rough times. He came back to church, served a full-time mission, and is now married in the temple to a beautiful returned missionary. Again, Heavenly Father uses us as instruments in His hands to help gather His sheep. And sometimes we don't even realize we are doing it.

Back in the singles ward, I began to pray constantly to have the desire to start over again and to find my true eternal mate. I dated many different wonderful people but knew that I wanted someone who truly honored his priesthood, loved his family, loved the Lord, prayed, went to the temple, fulfilled his callings in church, was a hard worker, respected me, and, most importantly, wanted to raise an eternal family in the church. These are all things that we are taught in Young Women, but I never realized how important they were until I settled for less and my first marriage fell apart.

I was so lucky to find such a person. I have been blessed to find such an amazing person. We were married for time and eternity in the temple and now have four beautiful children. Our marriage is not always perfect, but we are both striving for the same goals. We continue to pray together and trust in the Lord for help and guidance.

I also have wonderful friends who have helped me through many hard times. Women are strong when we trust in the Lord. These friends helped me through the hardest time of my life. I am sure there will be more, and I am glad to know they will always be there with me. We carry each other's burdens, cry with each other, fast and pray with each other, talk, and understand one another.

When I was married the first time, I believe the Spirit did tell me I was doing the right thing by getting married. I still believe that I was meant to go through the trials and tribulations that I did and that I was blessed to have had them. One day you may look on your life and think, "This is not what I had planned." It helps to think that it may have been planned long before we experienced it. Be grateful that you are one of the chosen, because "after much tribulation come the blessings. Wherefore the day cometh that ye shall be crowned with much glory; the hour is not yet, but is nigh at hand" (D&C 58:4).

3

The Coping Tool

I have a coping tool. It's a visual of me sitting with my best girlfriends in the pre-mortal existence. We're about to embark on our earthly journeys; but before we go, we're handed clipboards with various trials we can experience in our soon-to-be physical state. Knowing challenges result in becoming more Christlike, we eagerly begin considering which trials we'd like to endure. Some of us opt for smaller trials, because they can act as gentle reminders of our humble state. Apparently I checked some of those, including being uncoordinated, being unable to develop any real talent, and fear of speaking in church. Some of us decided that by selecting trials of greater significance, we would be catapulted to an even deeper understanding and appreciation of Christ. These trials would be life altering and would leave us in the depths of despair. Divorce fell into this category. I checked that one . . . twice.

My first temple marriage lasted all of one year. The odds were against us. Our parents were not supportive of us getting married. I was young. He was a medical student who one day declared he wasn't 100% sure there really was a God. Though in retrospect the dissolution of this marriage could be compared to a bad break-up from a college sweetheart, it was devastating. I got a severe dose of heartache, depression, insomnia, and embarrassment that made me want to spend all day in bed. Reluctantly, I made myself attend a weekly institute class—the one for singles (sigh)—visit the temple once a week, and stay active in my new young single adult ward (humbling, indeed). It took some time, but being where you're supposed to be and doing what you're supposed to do got me out of my slump.

At age 26, I married in the temple for the second time. Husband #2 and I should have worked out. We were mature enough, we meshed spiritually, we enjoyed similar interests . . . yet our relationship was lacking. I can't put my finger on exactly what decayed this marriage; but, seven years and two children later, husband #2 asked for a divorce. I was surprised but not shocked. I was blessed with superwoman powers as I sought legal counsel, put the house on the market, potty-trained my two-year-old, and took intermittent breaks to nurse my four-month-old.

Now age 33 and divorced twice, my self-esteem was severely deflated. But I had little time to feel sorry for myself. While busy creating a new life with my young children, I was prodded by a friend to "check out the possibilities" on an LDS social network. Scrolling through the site, I recognized several faces: girls who were once in my class when I was their Beehive Advisor. This only reminded me of my pathetic state. Finally, my eyes froze on a familiar name. It was an old flame I dated briefly after my first divorce. Hesitantly, I sent him a message. He responded somewhat embarrassed because he was 36 and still not married; he joked that he must not be the marrying type. I replied that I must not be the marrying type, either, since I was now divorced twice. That broke the ice. We eventually got married in the temple; and, I have to admit, there's truth to the cliché, "third time's a charm."

Shortly after getting married, an elderly and highly revered sister in my ward leaned over to me in Relief Society and whispered, "See, it all worked out. Plus, your new husband is so much better looking than the other one" (insert smile and wink).

This was a defining moment for me. Of course it would all work out; it always will. As I mentally took inventory of the trials I had endured thus far from my pre-mortal checklist, we began to sing our opening song: "Come, Ye Disconsolate." The words, by Thomas Moore, swelled in my heart: "Earth has no sorrow that heav'n cannot heal . . . Earth has no sorrow that heav'n cannot cure . . . Earth has no sorrow but heav'n can remove."

4

Fairy Tales

Women are programmed for romance and love. We grow up on storybook fairy tales and continue to tune into Hollywood's fairy tales where "happily ever after" is the rule, regardless of the obstacles presented. We accept this as reality and then wonder why our lives don't end happily ever after like a fairy tale.

Our generation has lost some of the lessons that the more gruesome versions of the fairy tales and fables were designed to teach. In previous generations, fairy tales were an oral tradition used to instruct children in fantastical and sometimes frightening ways to impress upon young minds the principles and virtues necessary to help them become better people. Children were taught what could happen if they didn't recognize the villains in their lives, the dangers around them, or the consequences of foolish choices. Instead, fairy tales have now become whimsical, lacking the infusion of wisdom that once made the stories more meaningful and applicable. The following are some of my personal fairy tales gone awry, including foolish choices of my own and others that are hopefully infused with hard-earned wisdom and the ever-important moral that makes my story one to learn from.

Snow White

I became somewhat aware of my problem of viewing life as a fairy tale when I was a freshman in college, living on campus. I had a boyfriend, and one day ran away from him just so he would pursue and capture me, like a scene from a fairy tale. He followed me for a minute but became disenchanted with the game and quit the chase, leaving me, the would-be princess, wholly dissatisfied.

At the time, I was a bit of a Snow White. After biting into the poisonous apple handed to me by dysfunctional "villains" of past and present, I wasn't awake enough to see what was really happening. I was too busy dreaming. I had gotten out of the proverbial woods of a very challenging upbringing, but I didn't realize that idealizing was the coping mechanism I used to keep me safe from the harsher realities of life. Ironically, the dreams didn't let me see clearly enough to make better choices to create the happily ever after I so desperately wanted.

After four years of chasing the "man of my dreams," I married my prince in the temple. But shortly after our honeymoon, I was awakened from my fairy-tale dream to the reality that my Prince was not-so-Charming after all. His constant berating over the smallest details, such as the right and wrong way to clean a refrigerator crisper drawer, took a heavy toll.

Soon, I was alone, blinded and blinking in the harsh light of reality, wondering how it had happened. I received the would-be reviving kiss at the altar, only to find I had to annul a destructive marriage and was without prince or crown.

Cinderella

My next fairy tale did not end happily ever after, either. I was older and wiser, with a good deal of college finished and a mission experience to boot. My new prince and I started off in typical fairy-tale fashion: a chance meeting in France, a spiritual confirmation that he was "the one," a whirlwind storybook romance, and a wedding in the temple for time and eternity. This had to be it, I thought. I got the prince and the castle and the promise of forever. I had escaped my upbringing and was now living happily with a husband and children I adored.

Then one day I learned that some princes who grow up with crowns don't always appreciate their kingdoms. The desire for conquest can become an obsession, and sadly, my prince took his quest for more into dangerous territory. As he made choices that violated our marriage covenants, he went on a path that has been both painful and damaging to our family. Within a few short years, our family suffered the pain of infidelity, excommunication, divorce, addiction, and abuse. I have often wondered how a family like ours could suffer such a torrent after what had started out so right. It's true that we write our own endings, but sometimes our co-authors take our stories a direction we never intended to go.

The Frog Prince

Reeling from the aftermath of divorce and wholly vulnerable, I hastily kissed a frog hoping he would turn into a prince. I was disenchanted with "ideal" men who came from seemingly ideal circumstances. I thought maybe if I didn't marry a prince, he could become one with enough of my love and support. So I married a man that was very compatible with me in many ways, in spite of some issues that I believed were surmountable. We had a lot in common: similar upbringings, compatible interests, and some shared values.

But not long after this marriage, I came to realize that part of my attraction to my current husband was that he was a lot like my own father, whose prototype I now realized I had tried (and failed) to escape in my first two marriages. Over the years I had come to accept that I couldn't change my father. I was now ready to admit that I couldn't change my princes, either. My biggest error in judgment was probably believing that we wanted the same things. It turned out we did not, and the discrepancy jeopardized our entire family. My husband was hiding pernicious addictions and a destructive streak with no real desire to change. No magical kiss from me would be powerful enough to pull off the transformation needed to go from frog to prince.

The Not-so-Happy but Hopeful Ending

These experiences came at a high price. My family has been deeply injured. I lost my bearings and felt completely shattered. Tragically, I physically and spiritually lost my daughter for three years after she was driven out of our home by my third husband. She escaped to live with her father but was subjected to abuse stemming from his addictions. Children, I sadly concede, are the real losers in such family trauma.

To my delight she has since come back to me. We are still not out of the briar patch, but we are learning how to nurse and heal our wounds and how to avoid injury in the future. We are learning how to become healthy and whole on our own so that we can be healthy and whole with someone else. We are also learning how to become good judges of character. I do believe there are valiant princes out there, and I trust I will find mine and marry again for eternity. I still believe every girl is a princess. This is what I choose to teach my daughter. I owe it to her to teach her how to choose a good man and how to be a strong woman deserving of such a man.

The Moral of My Story

From my first would-be prince I experienced abuse; and from my second, addiction and infidelity. And apparently, since I had not learned my lesson from the first two, with my third husband I experienced all three. The root of his problems, I was told, was sexual addiction. But more importantly, I discovered that the root of mine was that I was attracted to men like my father: a man I grew up loving but who had destructive and deep-rooted issues that I simply couldn't understand as a child and hadn't extracted myself from as an adult.

This forty-five-year experience has taught me much about abuse and recovery. I grew up determined to escape the abuse I experienced as a child; but so powerful was the conditioning of my early years, I didn't see abuse for what it was. And when I did, I didn't know the way out. I couldn't see and avoid the signs of addiction, abuse, and infidelity. I wanted to see roses, so I looked through rose-colored glasses and ended up grabbing at thorns.

I still look for roses, though. The roses I see now are my hope and faith in something and someone better with whom I can share my life. The thorns are still there, but my vision is clearer now; I recognize the thorns when I see them, and I'm not afraid to look for a different rose.

Sometimes I still feel foolish and deride myself for making choices that turned out to be so damaging. Forgiving ourselves is often as hard or harder than forgiving others. I try to remember that the choices I made were the best I could do at the time with what I had been given. For whatever reason, abuse has been a long-standing part of my life; but now, so is the precious knowledge of how to recover from it, shun it from my life, and teach others to do the same.

All around me I see wounded victims of similar fates. I feel compassion for them and try to help, but I will not be one of them again. I have learned to set healthy boundaries, and I am teaching my children how to do the same. It is a triumph to be able to teach them now what I did not know then. I can only pray that they will make choices that will lead them to their happily ever afters. I hope they will be a new generation of loving, healthy people, no longer plagued by the pain of infidelity, addiction, and abuse.

My Happy Ending

I have found an unexpected joy in healing. I have found joy in taking my outdated career skills and college diploma and re-inventing myself as an early-education teacher. It is a work I love; and I am a better teacher because of my experiences. I know how to help the children I teach in the difficult issues they already face.

I feel joy when I see my daughter healing from the abuse she has suffered. She has come to accept that she was not the cause or deserving of the abuse she received. She is slowly blossoming in her renewed faith in God and has put aside the suicidal thoughts and depression that threatened to engulf her. She will graduate from high school with honors and has turned away from choices made while she was snagged on thorns. She has done make-up work to achieve her four-year Seminary diploma, Young Women's medallion, and honor bee. She is entering college this fall, committed to getting her degrees and certificates to teach elementary school children. She has a goal to raise abuse awareness and already recognizes signs of disability and abuse in young children. She hopes to use this skill as a teacher who can assist with early intervention.

I feel joy when I see my son entering middle school already learning how to manage unhealthy situations with peers in his school. He has learned that he can be friendly to all without investing in unhealthy relationships. He is recognizing what is workable in a relationship and what is not. He has also come out of depression and is motivated. He graduated from elementary school with academic honors. He has earned his Cub Scout Arrow of Light and has set a goal to become an Eagle Scout. He plans to participate in sports and extracurricular events and is committed to getting the grades that will earn him a scholarship to college.

I share these accomplishments not to boast but to give hope to those who worry about their loved ones suffering from the ravages of abuse and/or divorce. Our family is living proof that God loves his children and that it is possible for a family to recover from the effects of abuse, addiction, infidelity, and divorce. Loving, inspired people, along with professional help have helped to make it possible. But most of all, our family has been healed through our faith in Heavenly Father and his son Jesus Christ, the real Prince of Peace.

In my house hangs a sign that says, "It is never too late to live happily ever after." Of this happy ending I am sure.

5

Staying True, Staying Strong

I have always been a very strong person—and sometimes a strong-willed person. I was born that way. Even at my wedding, my minister father encouraged my groom to find a way to "work together" with me because, as he said, "My daughter has a mind of her own." So I know I am not perfect, but I also know that I try hard, give everything I have to the things that matter to me, and don't quit easily.

I am a teacher in my community. I have worked hard to be a respected teacher and to be a role model to my students. One day at school, a parent commented to me that she was concerned about a man she had seen yelling at me in front of my school. I was embarrassed to admit that man was my husband.

When I married my husband, it was for keeps. I did not go into my marriage with the attitude that if it didn't work out I would just leave. I am a loyal person. I took my marriage vows and commitment very seriously for the entire seventeen years we were married. My husband was a very likeable person, was respected by people, and had a great sense of humor. I was attracted to him from the very first time I saw him. While we dated for a year before we got engaged, much of that was spent living 200 miles apart and seeing each other only sporadically. I realize now we did not know each other well enough to make that decision. I really did not know the day-to-day person that I married. Even though we were married for seven years without children, we neglected to get to know each other well enough to have a strong connection upon which to build a family. We each worked a lot and occasionally even took separate vacations. At the time I did not think this was odd; but once we started our family, I could see this was an unhealthy pattern.

Our first child, a blue-eyed, vivacious blonde, was a life-changer for me. Suddenly everything revolved around our beautiful baby girl. It was a difficult adjustment for my husband to not have my undivided attention. I hoped he would warm up to the wonderful change in our family, but it did not seem to get easier for him.

Our second child was a robust baby boy. I thought that his gender might encourage my husband to take more interest, but that was not the case. He still found things to do after work in order to not spend time with the family. Most nights he would not come home until late at night. "Visiting clients" or "getting in a work-out" were typical excuses. We both continued to work full time, but the care of the children was left almost entirely to me. Cooking, cleaning, baths, bedtime stories, and going to church were my responsibilities alone.

After a few years of living like this, I began to suspect my husband was having an affair. He denied it but suggested nonetheless that we separate. He eventually got around to confirming the affair. Strangely, of all days to tell me, he chose Mother's Day. At best it was poor planning; at worst it was cruel. I felt sick to my stomach and like my whole world was crashing in on me. I couldn't talk or even breathe. He tried to calm me down, but he was the last person I could listen to in that moment. I asked him to leave. From then on, I was alone with my children. Catastrophic as this felt, I had to pull myself together for my children. They were so innocent, and to whatever extent I could control, I didn't want this to affect their lives. They were only two years and eight months old, respectively.

Over the next year, the two of us worked hard to repair our marriage. We went to a counselor and took things slowly. Some things improved, and we got back together. We had our third child, a beautiful brown-eyed baby girl. But not everything changed.

My life was about caring for our kids. I wish I could say that our life was each other and our kids, but that had never been the case. My husband was an absent father by choice. I continued to work and essentially raise the children on my own. I longed for his support, his help, his acknowledgment. I remember a day when he left home blandly calling out, "Love you" to me. It felt hollow, and I felt no love in return. We tried counseling three different times, and I'm glad we did so that I could know I had tried. But in the end, certain injuries couldn't or wouldn't be repaired.

My husband's behavior became erratic and careless towards me and our children. In fits of temper he was known to drive recklessly and once abandoned my children and I in the car in an undesirable neighborhood without keys or cell phone. Still not ready to give up on our marriage, I did not leave; but not long afterwards, my husband filed for divorce. He had my divorce papers served to me at school in hopes of humiliating me in front of my students, and I was humiliated. I stood in my classroom stunned and in disbelief.

I tried to convince my husband that we needed more time to try to repair our relationship; but he was done, and I was too emotionally exhausted to continue the fight. After almost seventeen years, I gathered the children and moved out. It was the hardest and most frightening thing I have ever done. The only relief I felt was not living in uncertainty, anymore. I still hoped my husband might reconsider, but it did not seem likely. We both had too much anger to find workable ground again.

Friends encouraged me to "move on," but how do you do that with three young children and a full-time job? How do you find the time to work on yourself? Where do you go for answers in navigating this new life you didn't anticipate? Counseling helped some; but on top of the pain, I just felt confused. Nothing felt "normal" or familiar.

The new normal would take a long time to create. One major step toward it was buying a new house for myself and my children. I worked hard to make it our home: a secure, safe, peaceful home. I continued to keep our children involved in outside activities and took them to church. We traveled with friends and family to places we had never been before. I tried to make their lives as normal as possible, continuing on with their sporting events, recitals, and parties. I took my kids on adventures, and we started having fun again. We loved and trusted each other. We felt like a team. Instead of seeing only the negatives of my life since the divorce, I started to concentrate on all the good in my life, instead.

I had a lot of support through this difficult time; and the most helpful people were those who listened and offered a shoulder to cry on. It was not their advice that made the difference but their encouragement and moral support. Helping me laugh through it all was so healing. Allowing me to cry was so necessary. Those first few years after my divorce, I clung to family and friends, and it saved my life. An important step in my growth was doing things I never thought I could do; but with the love of family and friends, I found the strength.

Vacations became an important source of relief. Family vacations now meant my children and I going with my family, my sisters, or our friends. One year my entire family took a vacation to Yellowstone National Park, all going in separate motor homes. I had never done anything like this by myself. I rented a motor home for my kids and me and traveled with my family in a caravan from our home state all the way there. The sense of accomplishment was overwhelming. If I could do this, I could do anything. Through adventures like this, I learned to trust myself again. I began to trust my decisions and my ability to provide a good life for myself and my children.

I often wonder how I made it through those first few years. Living through the death of a relationship that I thought would be the most important of my life was traumatic. Continuing the relationship with my ex-husband as parents of our children continued to be a difficult and sad reminder of our painful past. I learned that like everything in life, people change and relationships change. It takes both spouses to make a marriage work. It takes both partners keeping their marriage vows, being trustworthy, acting like partners, and remaining loyal and faithful to each other. We were missing most if not all of those elements. In the end, the wounds from my husband's infidelity turned out to be too deep for either of us to recover from.

There are never guarantees that a person you love won't hurt you or leave you. You love and give and trust the best you can. And there still may come a time when you have to rely on your strength alone to get you through. Fortunately, I never really was alone. My deepest source of strength came from my own faith and God's many tender mercies as He carried me through my dark storm. I believe in a Father that loves His children so much that He never separates himself from them, even when things go so terribly wrong and the light of day is not visible. There were times I wanted to blame God for my circumstances and misfortunes, but I learned that there is a greater purpose for each of us on this earth. I have become a stronger person because of my journey, and the Lord has been there for me to give me the strength, endurance, and faith to keep going. Maybe that was my lesson, to know my Creator and myself more intimately. To know that He is always there for me, and for all of us. I know now that I am never alone, and He will always be there with me and for me.

More than eleven years have now passed since our divorce. My ex-husband married a good woman, which has been a blessing for me and my children. All three of our children are now in college, preparing to live their lives on their own. I hear from my children daily, and I am happy that they still come to me for advice and help. I take comfort knowing I have done my best with my children under less-than-ideal circumstances. My children are strong, independent, and loving. Raising them as a divorced mom was not easy, but I worked hard to be the best example I could be to them. They know their mom is always there for them.

I still teach and find great satisfaction making a difference in my students' lives. I have taken on new challenges as a home and hospital teacher, which has enriched my life and gives me new opportunities to help others. Because of what I have been through, I enjoy working with students and families through very challenging times. The lessons I learned and strength I gained from my experiences live on to bless the lives of others going through their hard times.

I feel like a different person now. I am still strong and confident; but just as important, I am more caring and compassionate. I take what I have learned and use it as I teach, encourage, and inspire my own children, my family, my students, and people I interact with every day. I love my children and thank God that even though they came from a marriage that did not survive, they came through it to be confident, healthy young adults. I thank Him also that I survived, and I am happy to say I like who I have become.

6

Slow and Steady

One day my mother called unexpectedly to warn me about a premonition she had had regarding a potential threat to my safety. Her warning, while dramatic, was not entirely unwarranted, given the state of my relationship with my husband at that time. I had recently learned of his pornography addiction coupled with an extramarital affair; however, in what felt like a strange reversal, it was he who was intensely angry at me.

The warning from my mother was simple and direct: "Do not go boating on the lake with your husband today." I respected my mother's intuition but, believing others would be present, felt assured of my safety. The details are not pleasant to recount; but at the end of the day, I found myself abandoned in the middle of a large lake with no life preserver, very little ability to swim, and a phobia of fish.

The weeks leading up to this day had not been happy ones. I had neither slept nor eaten much, and anxiety consumed me most of the time. Notwithstanding all of that, the moment I watched my husband leave me to drown in the middle of that lake was, without a doubt, when I hit rock bottom. How I wished I had listened to my mother. How I wished this was not my life. In this, my darkest hour, I turned to God and pleaded for His help. "Heavenly Father," I cried, "I need you more than ever. Please help me!" Into my panicked mind came the words, "slow and steady." They were unmistakable; and yet, in my distress, I could not see how *slow* or *steady* would be enough to save me from this hopeless plight. I was too far from shore and too inexperienced a swimmer. But I put my trust in God. He would have to help me. Slowly and steadily I swam, then floated—front, then back. When I thought I could not go any further, His voice in my mind urged me on, *slow and steady,* until I reached the dock. I had lived a miracle. In the absence of an orange life vest on that desperate afternoon, the Lord was my life preserver.

Sadly, struggle and heartache still lay ahead as I neared the dock only to watch my husband unload the boat and drive away in his truck without saying a word. He had to have understood the gravity and callousness of what I had just endured at his hands, but his heart was cold and clearly beyond feeling any degree of tenderness for me.

I tried to be thankful I was alive, but my rejoicing gave way to despair as the knowledge of how my husband really felt about me sunk deep into the crevices of my already broken heart. Not knowing how to make sense of my painful realizations, I called my mom. Sad as she was that her premonition had come to fruition, she tried to comfort me and counseled me to seek safety.

I learned an unforgettable lesson that day. I learned that promptings from the Spirit are real and can protect us from danger, but only to the degree that we heed them. When life crowds out our clarity and is replaced by fear or anger, it is easy to dismiss or downplay the warnings of the Spirit. We do so at our peril, sometimes physically, always spiritually. Fortunately for me, and probably most of us, when we do not listen the first time, the Lord is merciful with second chances. When hope seemed lost, I put my trust in the Lord and kept moving; and *slowly* but *steadily,* he delivered me. My deliverance from the lake that afternoon would turn out to be a type for other miraculous deliverances yet to come.

Thus began my attempt to recover and rebuild my life after divorce. Prayer and fasting became a staple in my life. I began the difficult work of creating a new life, a new home, and trying to find new strength. Each step was marked with struggle. Perhaps the greatest price, however, was watching my children choose to believe malicious and untrue accusations against me. Some of my own children chose not to speak to me any longer. I felt helpless against a man who was living two lives and seemed to be getting the best of each life, while I seemed to be getting only the worst.

This was a time of great confusion and angst; and besides my own uncertainty, I worried about getting my youngest daughter settled in a home and school that could give her much-needed stability. I had fasted and prayed for direction but had received no answers. That night I read the Bible story of Gideon to my daughter and her cousins before bed and was struck by the relevance of the message for me. Gideon was unsure of whether to go to battle, so he asked for a sign. If he was to go to battle, the Lord was to make a fleece that Gideon had put on the ground be dry while the grass was wet with dew in the early morning. The next day he asked that the fleece could be wet but the grass dry. Both times, God granted his wish, and Gideon was satisfied that God knew him and heard him. I longed for a Gideon experience of my own.

I hoped my request would not offend the Lord, but I hoped that in His mercy He would grant me direction and an assurance that He was aware of me. I approached the Lord with the question of whether I should move to a certain town I had been considering. That particular town had a temple, which was a powerful draw for me, but I felt the need for guidance beyond my own wisdom. Like Gideon, I decided upon the sign I desired. Several months earlier, I had found a home in a town that I adored but was unable to purchase at that time. My realtor assured me this house would not be on the market more than a week or two, but I hadn't been able to stop thinking about it. I decided that if that house was still for sale that would be my sign that this was the right move for me. I inquired and to my delight, the house had not sold. I had my sign! I had asked the Lord and He had answered! I was humbled and grateful; but for reasons I could not understand, I did not feel peace about buying that house.

I was now second-guessing both whether I really wanted the house and whether my sign was really a sign. Did I want to live this far from my hometown? Would this be a good school and neighborhood for my daughter? Would I find friends and the support I needed? Doubts bombarded me and, once again, confusion and anxiety overwhelmed me. Then the thought came to me, *Gideon asked for a second sign.* I was already feeling a little guilty, although grateful, for my first sign, so I tried to resist the temptation to ask for a second but ultimately gave in. I simply wanted to know the Lord's will; and I had always believed that if we ask, He will answer. My answer came in a way I did not expect. After a closer inspection of the first house, I realized it did not offer the things I needed for my daughter and myself. I now understood why I lacked peace. Still, the Lord surely had some purpose in leading my heart to this town. A bit sheepishly, I now asked Heavenly Father to provide us with a different home in this town, in a good neighborhood, at the end of a quiet street, with a yard, and (if possible) the southern exposure I thrive on. I knew it seemed like a lot to ask, but it was what I most desired for my daughter and myself.

Having dared to ask, I ventured out to find a home similar to the first but closer to our needs. Despite seeing every available home in the area, my realtor found nothing that fit our needs. "What do I do now?" I thought. I turned down my first sign only to ask for another and received no answer. Not exactly the Gideon experience I had hoped for. After a day of house hunting with my realtor, I had planned to go to the temple, hoping to get some direction or clarity there. At the end of the day my diligent realtor took us back to her office for one final search on the computer. As I prepared to leave her office, she called out, "Wait a minute. This is it!" and printed out a new listing.

She took me to a house that was everything I had dreamed of and more: A beautiful home on a hill overlooking the city, on a quiet cul-de-sac, with a huge yard for my daughter, a sledding hill, the southern exposure I longed for, and even a pool! It was perfect for us. Except for the price. Reality set in quickly when I learned that the asking price, which had already been lowered $20,000, was still out of my range. Having nothing to lose, I made an outrageously low offer comprising a small down payment and modest monthly rent until I could get more money together. I topped it off with a bold request to move in within four days so that my daughter could start school in our new home. The realtor laughed. She knew better than to think such an outlandish offer would be taken seriously. This house, she said, could easily fetch more than twice my proposed rent amount, and no one moved in sooner than thirty days. I asked her to try anyway and left her with my testimony of a loving God who I know watches over all mothers.

The next day my realtor, still in shock, called with news that my offer had been accepted. She was astounded. I was elated. Within four days, I was moved in, and my daughter was on time for her first day of class in a wonderful grade school a few blocks down the hill.

God had watched over me. He continues to watch over me. His love has kept me going. Divorce, like many trials, often comes at a high cost. For a long time loss overwhelmed me. *Slowly and steadily* I have faced each day since my divorce, finding the strength to swim safely to shore and the courage to ask for a miracle from Heavenly Father, who has never left my side.

In some ways my story is unique. I don't make it a practice to ask the Lord for signs and miracles, and I know that luxuries are not typical compensation for our trials. And I hope I would be as grateful whether or not I were in my dream home. But often, and sometimes when we need it most, our Heavenly Father pours out more blessings than we can imagine. If we will simply turn to Him and try our best, even if our best is *slow but steady*, He will give us every needful thing, and then some.

7

Surviving and Thriving

Life as a convert to my new church was exciting. I had been asked to be a missionary over the youth groups, which is where I met my husband-to-be. The fact that we were both converts gave us something in common, and things moved quickly from there. Six months later, we were married in a church ceremony. I then supported him through six years of schooling, after which he got a job as a professor at a junior college. We moved to a new town and bought a home. Everything felt right, and we were off to a wonderful start.

After almost twenty years of marriage, my husband and father of our six children (ranging from 3 to 15 years), decided that he would be happier not being married to me. He left me and our children and immediately began divorce proceedings. Six weeks later, one of my church leaders innocently asked me how I was dealing with my husband's remarriage. "His what?" was all I could utter. I was in shock. I did not even know that our divorce was final, let alone that he had been seeing someone else—and married her. My church leader regretted being the one to tell me. She assumed that I must have known this fact. It was just one of many secrets I was not to be privy to regarding my husband.

I learned that our divorce had indeed been finalized a few days earlier, somehow without me present or even knowing. Three days after that my now ex-husband remarried. It was a lot for me and my children to process. To add insult to injury, my ex-husband and his new wife moved in two blocks east of us. Much too close for comfort. It was convenient for the kids, but their unfriendliness toward me was painful. I supposed their own guilt was the reason behind their unkindness to me, but that didn't help much to take away the sting.

Perhaps I should not have been so surprised by this development, given that my husband's track record was less than perfect. Five years earlier, he had been excommunicated from our church for having an affair with one of his college students. He lost his church membership as well as his job, our only source of income. I learned to forgive and gave him a second chance. He found other jobs, and we went on as best we could, adding two more children to our family. Thinking back, I should have seen the red flags, but we make the best decisions we can with the information we have. And for many of us, hoping for better days is how we cope and move on. But better days did not come right away. I found myself devastated and divorced, a single mother with six children. How we would survive I did not know, but despite the scars I knew we would—and we did!

What is now important from my story is what I have to share to help someone else survive a similar trial or, even better, avoid it altogether. Here then are a few of my lessons learned.

1. *Date smarter.* Our engagement was not long enough to really get to know each other. We lived over an hour apart and both had full-time jobs. We needed more time to court and to talk. Our communication skills were nearly nonexistent. We did not know how to have a discussion without putting the other in a defensive mode. We lacked problem-solving skills with one another and never learned how to resolve life's problems together. Our knowledge of and ability to talk

about intimate marital relations was low and prevented us from truly bonding with each other. Neither of us understood much about the other, especially in terms of how men and women think and approach certain things differently. There were no premarital classes in our area, and neither of us got much tutelage from our parents. These things simply weren't talked about back then. They should be.

2. *Date after marriage.* My husband and I rarely spent free time together. After work, my husband preferred to play ball with his friends or go to a college basketball game on his own. When he was home, he could typically be found behind a newspaper while I ran the affairs of the house. In my anger and hurt, I responded by giving him the silent treatment, which I now see did not help matters. I relied on the belief that he loved our children enough that no matter how I acted, he would never leave. I was wrong. Marriage needs attention, time, talk, and togetherness. These things foster friendship and affection, which we desperately needed but didn't know how to create. One Sunday, we asked a happily married woman to come and speak to our youth group. She told the group that whenever she heard the garage door opening, her heart would start to pound at the thought that her husband was home. They were very much in love. I felt so sad that I did not feel this way toward my husband. I mistakenly thought I just didn't love my husband, anymore. I wish I'd realized that love grows out of shared experiences and kindness. Instead of pulling together, we drifted apart, each becoming less and less invested in each other. To fill the resulting void, I turned to my relationships with my children. My husband turned to extramarital relationships and, ultimately, to the one that would end our marriage.

3. *Trust your instincts.* After my husband left me, I remember wondering how I would ever raise six children on my own. The thought seemed overwhelming and not doable. I wondered if we wouldn't be better off separating the children so that

three lived with him and three lived with me. My husband
agreed, but a good friend and lawyer counseled me that my
children would likely feel alienated from each other and like
distant cousins more than siblings. They had lost enough
family without more separation. I knew in my gut that the
children must stay together. My husband disagreed angrily,
but I held my ground. A few years later, my oldest son gave
me a wonderful multi-picture framed wall hanging with a
beautiful quote from the scriptures, "Having their hearts knit
together in unity and in love one towards another." I knew
I had done the right thing for my children. They needed the
closeness and strength of each other, which they never would
have enjoyed if we had raised them separately from each
other. Always listen to your heart and your instincts; they
always tell you the truth.

4. *Allow others to grieve with you.* I delayed telling my parents
about my divorce until they came out for their yearly visit.
After three days of making excuses for my absent ex-husband,
I broke down and told them. They were naturally furious
with him. I told them not to be mad, because we were coping
quite well; but it was natural for my parents to be upset.
Divorce not only affects the immediate family, but extended
family, friends, and everyone that is a part of your life. In
that sense, no one suffers alone—and letting others in can be
healing for everyone.

5. *Embrace change.* When I finally came to terms with the fact
that my husband had left for good, I cleaned out the entire
two-car garage. It was liberating in terms of gaining both
physical space and emotional space. I decided to fill that newly
claimed space with gear for something our family enjoyed
doing but hadn't done for so long: camping. That weekend
I took all six kids camping. Walking in the mountains and
along streams was so calming. Camping as a family became

a renewed tradition, one that went on to give us a much-needed sense of security and joy of togetherness. It became a true bonding time, forging deep connections even after the kids got married years later. Nature helps with healing, and so do traditions.

6. *Trust that things will work out.* My ex-husband agreed to pay for our children's missions and college educations, but he never did. Nonetheless, all three of my sons served missions, and some have gone to college. Thanks to the help of wonderful people in our church, all of the things that matter were taken care of. For my part, I worked my hardest to provide every needful thing for my children. At one point, I worked three part-time jobs. The older kids helped out more. We rented out our downstairs to bring in extra money. I baked and sold nearly 100 loaves of bread each week. I shopped at thrift stores. We put our trust in the Lord, and things did work out.

Looking back almost thirty years, I wonder how I made it through the raw emotion, sadness, and financial strain, while trying to be both parents, being angry at not being able to joy in the children's graduations and marriages together, and so many other losses and disappointments. It was a very hard time, and there was no easy way around it. The only soothing balms I found were my knowledge of Christ's love and Atonement and our understanding that He did suffer for us—not only for sins we can repent of, but also the grief, wounds, and hardships we endure through life.

Having this knowledge, my church, and a few wonderful friends who stood by me through it all, helped me go from merely surviving to thriving. I realized that I am the author of how I feel, and nothing outside of myself can make me happy or sad without my consent. This realization has helped me to see that only I hold the keys to how I deal with what life gives me. As hard as it gets, I turn to my faith and the wonders of the earth that surround me. This brings me calm, fills my reservoir, and allows me to thrive.

8

What About Children's Voices?

The night my children and I learned that their father had unexpectedly remarried only six weeks after our divorce, my oldest son, then thirteen, came to me with his two little brothers in tow and asked, "Does this mean that Dad is not our dad, anymore?" I assured them that their dad would always be their dad, but my heart broke for their shaken perceptions of their place and importance in their own family.

Soon after that, my fifth child's schoolteacher informed me that she had noticed a deep sadness in my daughter. This was accompanied by stomachaches. I concluded that my daughter was suffering from the divorce by keeping her feelings and sadness inside.

When yet another child asked if Dad would ever come back to live with us, I was forced to answer "no." He would never come back to live with us again. My sweet daughter cried and cried but after that seemed to feel much better. Children need our permission to feel sad and express it. They have suffered a great loss at the break-up of their family and need a space to mourn and grieve and talk and cry.

My younger children paid a different price—not so much emotionally at the time, but in drastic disruptions to their daily lives. The need for me to return to work meant that my three-year-old had to attend day care, something I had hoped to avoid for all of my children.

Until this string of events, I had given too little thought to my children's feelings as they struggled to cope with losing their father in the home. I had been listened to by wonderful friends; and now to my sorrow, I realized that my children had not been given the same gift. I made a point to talk with each of my children and find out how they were feeling. I gave them permission to express themselves however they needed to. I only wish I had done it sooner and more often; but once I did, it opened the door to their healing.

At times, my ex-husband used one of our children as a confidante and a secret ally. This was terribly unfair to this child and put her in the difficult position of taking sides, which a child should never be forced to do.

Later, I came across some personal writings of my two oldest sons, in which they wrote of considering suicide. Tragically, each son thought that he was the reason for our divorce. I was so dreadfully unaware of their burdens and misconceptions! As parents, we must stay in tune with our children and help them through their pain. Looking back, I wish there had been more resources available in those days to help me know how to help them cope better. Too often they felt pressured to keep their feelings inside. I see so clearly now that talking and listening are the key to overcoming.

As they grew, our children's feelings toward their father varied. The older children do not harbor the resentment toward their father that the younger ones do, but all of our children, even as adults, have struggled to address their sadness and feelings with their father. Some of our children have confronted their father head-on in anger, some have had conversations with him, some have written letters to him, and some have yet to address it. It is a long process, and I know it takes courage to revisit that sad place. Perhaps like many spouses who choose to leave their family, my ex-husband's typical line of defense has been to justify his choice as one best for him and virtually harmless for everyone else. All my children really want to hear from him is an acknowledgment of the pain he brought to our family and an apology. "I'm sorry that I did this to you" would go a long way in their ability to make peace and move on.

But move on we must, if only by pushing ourselves forward. This past summer we had a family reunion. My oldest son encouraged me to invite their father. Even the thought made me recoil with a sickening feeling. I wondered why he would even ask such a thing of me. When I shared my unrest over it with a good friend, she suggested I attend the twelve-step program offered at our church for people with addictions. I wondered how an addiction program had anything to do with me, but at her encouragement I went. It did not take long for me to understand her suggestion. I realized that I was addicted to being a victim! I had lived so long as the one "wronged" that I had almost forfeited my ability to see myself through any other lens. This discovery was incredibly freeing for me. I felt lighter than I had in years. I came to realize that my ex-husband was likely never going to be sorry for his actions, but that didn't mean that I had to suffer from his foolishness forever! Christ had already atoned for my fears and anger and sorrow. After all these years, the power and ability to free myself from the negative feelings I still had towards him were right in front of me.

I took a leap of faith. I invited my ex-husband to our family reunion. I survived it, and our six children were glad of it. I did not doubt my children's feelings for me anymore. We had been through so much together, I knew our bond was sure. Together at the reunion their father and I celebrated our 70th birthdays as our children and twenty-three grandchildren interviewed us on tape talking about our lives. How far we had come!

Divorce affects generations and changes our children forever, therefore changing our posterity forever. We must keep our family close and our children our first priority, especially through divorce.

Their voices need to be heard, acknowledged, and answered by us as their parents. We owe them that. We must do our best to serve our children and help them grow up to be healthy, happy, well-adjusted adults. They helped me survive my darkest time, and together we help each other thrive.

9

Rowing Together

Looking back, I refer to this particular day in my life as "the Valentine's Day Massacre." I used to think that this was the day my world permanently changed. In reality, it had been changing slowly, incrementally, almost imperceptibly for years. Had I been less naïve, more experienced, and maybe even more cynical, I suppose that I could have seen the signs. But in reality, I didn't want to.

My husband, who was my college sweetheart and father of my four young children, and I were out for a Valentine's dinner when he announced that he was leaving me.

Several months prior to this, I could sense an emotional distancing between the two of us. I easily attributed it to the fact that he was under a lot of stress between trying to make partner at his firm, having four kids in seven years, and recently turning 40. If that's not a formula for a mid-life crisis, I'm not sure what is. Any one of these things might answer the question of why he was acting differently.

I began to notice that he seemed to avoid eye contact whenever possible. He would come home from work, give me an obligatory kiss on the cheek, and then keep busy playing with the kids. We felt more like roommates than spouses. With my last pregnancy, he was completely uninterested in choosing a name for the baby, feeling the baby kick, or anything that remotely connected "us." As I think back, I remember other red flags that slowly began to add up. On Christmas Day, I heard him having a private phone conversation behind closed doors. "Who could that be?" I mused, considering the fact that his entire extended family was present in our dining room. Another time, when I was pregnant and half asleep on the couch, I overheard him making plans to visit a local tourist attraction the next day when I thought he had to work. When the next Visa bill came, I wondered why were there two Tiffany necklaces on the statement, when I had only ever received one. And those free babysitting weekends we had won at a fundraising auction were never used for the getaway that I had imagined. I see now that would have required us to be together alone, which apparently was not a goal that we shared.

In spite of his plausible explanations, I continued to feel a very tangible emotional disconnect. It was a very unhappy and confusing time. His "favorite" little things no longer brought a smile to his face. He only seemed irritated that I was being nice to him. He encouraged me, almost overly so, to take a cooking class or go do something for myself. After finally connecting some of the dots, I remember telling my sister, "If I didn't know better, I would think that he was having an affair. I wouldn't rule that out, but I know that he would never cheat on the kids." Famous last words. I didn't want to add to his stress, but I finally wrote him a letter, enumerating all of the good things we had shared together, reminding him of what we used to be, and ultimately asking the question of what had happened to "us."

Valentine's Day was coming up, so I decided to plan an evening out. My husband was not all that romantic in the first place, but he was noticeably less so towards the end. Case in point: the year before, he had invited the entire Boy Scout troop over to our house on Valentine's Day. So, taking no chances of another Scout invasion, I set up a date, got a sitter, and made a reservation. We were going to focus on us, discuss the letter I had written, and get things back on track—or so I thought. I can still see every detail of that night in my mind. It was as surreal as if I were watching the events unfold on a movie screen, because it *had* to be happening to someone else, not me and my little family! This was not the way my life was supposed to be. I most definitely did not approve this script.

Dinner did not go well. When did we forget how to talk to each other? After an uncharacteristically awkward dinner came dessert. With dessert came the concise pronouncement from my husband and erstwhile best friend: "I'm not the person you think I am. I have been seeing someone else for quite some time. I've also been in therapy, and my therapist has been encouraging me to stop living a lie." So there, it was out. Three short sentences and my whole world careened off its axis, never to be the same. Life as I knew it was forever changed. My dazed response: "You've been going to therapy? How long, and why was I not a part of this?" My mind could not wrap around the larger issue. I could only muster, "Therapy? Who would have thought?" It was all so confusing. Who was this person sitting across from me, why were tears running down his face, and what had he done with my husband?

We quickly paid the check and left the restaurant, picking up the discussion in the car as we drove home. I had heard of accident victims going into shock, their minds protecting their bodies from registering the pain that they were in. This was the first of many tender mercies I would experience. It was as if unseen hands were protecting me from feeling or bearing the full impact of this unfathomable blow. This was the beginning of a whole new understanding of the Atonement. I remained eerily calm. My brain could hardly process the information. He said he wouldn't blame me if I threw him out that night. His parents were watching the kids. My thoughts raced, "I must hold it together, smile, and tell them thank you. Wait, what? Throw him out? Is he leaving? No, this cannot be happening. Together, we can fix it."

Strangely, I had an overwhelming feeling of compassion toward this man that I had known and loved for nearly twenty years. "Look at him. He's a wreck, a broken man," I thought to myself. "What can I say to convey to him that we are a team and no obstacle is too great, if we face it together? People survive things much worse than this and what do they do? They stand by each other and their challenges draw them closer. We have four little kids, practically babies. The oldest is just seven, the youngest not even one. We *have* to work it out." The alternative was simply unimaginable to me.

What I soon came to realize was that there was no turning the proverbial barge around; its course was set. We went to see his therapist together, who was the same brilliant character who told him to get in touch with his "inner child." Now I'm no doctor of psychology, but following the advice of one's so-called inner child did not ring the least bit true with my religious perspective or my common-sense philosophy of life. The waters were becoming muddy, and I wasn't sure what the truth was, anymore. Was it really that subjective?

After the counseling session where that sage piece of advice was proffered, another tender mercy occurred. I came home and, as my mind searched for sanity, I opened my scriptures. I randomly began to read in chapter three of Mosiah. Verse 19 reads:

> For the natural man is an enemy to God, and has been from the fall of Adam, and will be, forever and ever, unless he yields to the enticings of the Holy Spirit and putteth off the natural man and becometh a saint through the Atonement of Christ the Lord, and becometh as a child, submissive, meek, humble, patient, full of love, willing to submit to all things which the Lord seeth fit to inflict upon him, even as a child doth submit to his father.

It was amazing. "Ask and ye shall receive, knock and it shall be opened unto you"—the answer to the question in my heart was right there in black and white. This event was a turning point for me. Instant clarity. I received an immediate confirmation in my heart that *this* was the truth, and I could turn to the source of this truth whenever I needed answers. It provided both a fountain of knowledge and a refuge from the storm. I found myself going to this source often with a consistent result of enlightenment and comfort.

After a couple of fruitless counseling visits, it became quickly apparent that these sessions were not going yield my desired result. I hoped, I prayed, I wrung my hands. I wrote in my journal all of the eloquent points that I would make in our next session. I believed that my every word was crucial because, in my mind, that would change everything. If only I could just say the right thing, they would both see that I was right – we had to save our marriage, our family. After about the third visit, I realized that the two of them had no interest in giving hope to the marriage. They were merely trying to convince me that it was "best for us" to split up. To me it was a total waste of a hundred bucks an hour. I would never be convinced that this was the best and only path for our family. I wanted to scream, "Don't you understand? This is our *eternal family* that we are talking about here?"

I came from a divorced family, myself, and I had always dreamed of what it would be like to have my own family someday. I would have the family that I had always wanted. One factor that I had naively overlooked was that I couldn't maintain that family alone. I was only half of the equation. It would require the partnership and desire of both of us to work on our marriage and keep our family together. My determination was centered upon the fact that I was not only the voice for myself; I was also the voice for these four innocent children. I told myself that I would absolutely get through this, because God doesn't give us more than we can handle, right?

I was calm on the outside but crumbling on the inside. I fed the baby in her bouncy-seat, which I pushed into the corner so she wouldn't bounce the squash all over her face. Another added benefit to this feeding technique was that no one could see the tears silently rolling down my face as I looked into her wide-eyed, trusting gaze. I ran and ran. I was not a runner by any stretch of the imagination. I hated running, actually. But it was the one thing that made me feel as bad on the outside as I did on the inside. Between running and stress, I lost about twenty pounds in a couple of months. I cleaned. Maybe if I picked up the toys and the house were tidier. Maybe if I made lunches with notes inside. Maybe if I grew my hair longer, wore the right clothes, and put on mascara, even when it wasn't the weekend. Maybe there was something I could say or do that would flip the switch and turn the light back on. Maybe, maybe, maybe. No. Elvis had left the building, and no amount of love or determination was going to bring him back.

Hoping against hope that this really wasn't happening to me, I waited two agonizing weeks before telling a soul. As I left the bishop's office after meeting with him to share my burden, I felt as if a giant weight had been lifted from me. I went out to my car, sat in the empty parking lot, and sobbed tears of relief as I realized that I was not alone. An unexpected emotion also came to me: gratitude. I found my heart saying to the Lord, "Thank you for trusting me with this trial." Knowing that the Lord would not give us any trial greater than what we could handle, I felt that the Lord must have much more confidence in me than I had in myself. This gave me the self-assurance that I lacked.

When the news of our separation got around to our friends, devastation seemed to be the common theme. "You two are the perfect couple. If you can't make it, no one can." I could see that my very presence made people feel uncomfortable as they recognized their own vulnerability through me. Gradually, I began to process the new State of the Union. One day, as I was standing in a used bookstore, a cover caught my eye: *Dumped*. Yes, it hit me: this was my new reality. I bought the book, realizing even at the time that it was probably bad feng shui to have such a title on my shelf. But, as I skimmed through the pages, I felt a little better. The words leapt off the page: "Cheating spouses will vilify you to justify themselves." "They will say that they never loved you." "The affair is a symptom of a bigger problem, not the cause." These words resonated. They were talking about *me*! Other women were hearing these same lines. I was oddly relieved. I was not alone.

After about six weeks of playing emotional tug-of-war, my husband of fifteen years left. The weeks prior to the big event were some of the most tortuous weeks of my life. At my insistence, he delayed leaving until after our oldest daughter's baptism. I did not want this sacred milestone to be tainted by the memory of her father leaving. When the day I had been dreading finally came, in some ways it was almost a relief. It was easier to finally get on with it than hope for something that was clearly never going to be. Prior to breaking the news to our two oldest children, I told him that I would not lie to them and that I expected the same from him. He would have to tell them why he was leaving.

We went to a tiny, featureless park. There were no play structures to distract or lure us away from the task at hand. My then-husband said to the children, "Daddy is going to go live somewhere else. I just don't love Mommy anymore the way that two people should who are married." There were tears all around and protests aplenty to the tune of, "How can you not love Mommy anymore? Mommy is great." He replied, "Yes, Mommy is a great Mommy to you. But, I am making a choice that is right for me."

Again, I felt an odd sense of relief. All of my effort and energy had gone into avoiding this very moment—the moment he told our children these soul-crushing words. Now that it was out, I could focus on something more productive, something I had more control over, like making our new reality the best it could be. I would take this opportunity to set the stage for my children to have a different experience than I had when my own dad left. In desperation, my similarly blindsided mother asked us, "What are we going to do? *What are we going to do?*" This much I knew for sure: elementary school-age children do not have the answer to that question. Now, as an adult, it was going to be my job to figure out what to do.

Once I accepted the situation, pragmatism kicked in. Now what? For starters, I decided we would not be using the "D" word. To me, Divorce, with a capital "D," comes with a feeling of rejection, abandonment, and fault, with plenty of bitterness and choosing of sides thrown in. I knew firsthand that these are burdens that do not belong to children. Instead I would say, "Dad and I are no longer married." He would become "my kids' dad" instead of "my ex-husband." We would now be two families of five instead of one family of six. To some, it is only a matter of semantics, but to me, each message was significant. Regardless of our adult choices, my foremost goal was for the children to feel the love and security that every child deserves.

The day after the news, I asked my son how he felt about going off to kindergarten. Having been down this road myself at his age, I could relate to his candid response. He said, "I'm scared. I'm scared that I won't be like the other kids, anymore." I assured him that he would be like other kids—other kids who also had two parents who loved them but lived in separate homes.

My own dad's moving day came when I was almost five years old and just on my way to kindergarten. He began loading up his things while my mother and sister clung to each other by the stove, crying. My six-year-old brother and I numbly looked on. If ever there were an antithesis of a Norman Rockwell moment, this is one that would be indelibly etched into my mind. However, thanks to that snapshot, this would not be the legacy of my children. The day their dad moved out, there was no audience. We went to Grandma's house to play in the creek. When we came home, I told them that although their dad wasn't living with us anymore, he still loved them very much. We gathered in the family room where I hung a picture of Jesus, so aptly called the Savior. I remember telling the kids that they did not need to worry, because He was the head of our home. He would *always* be there for them and was *always* as close as a prayer.

I explained to the kids that when my parents divorced, we defaulted to an "every man for himself" strategy on what appeared to be a sinking ship. I then asked if they thought that we could get farther faster individually, or if we all got in the same boat and supported each other by rowing together. "Together," they replied in unison. I felt them holding on to every word as though their very world was hanging in the balance with each syllable. In a very real sense, it was. At times, I have felt like God's sock puppet, his message coming through me to my children. I asked for help and whenever I needed it most, I heard words beyond my own wisdom coming out of my mouth. I would have done anything to "fix it" if I could; but as that was no longer an option, I did my best to buffer them from the force of the storm.

Later, my five-year-old conveyed this message to his dad: "You are in your own boat, rowing by yourself, and you are not going to get very far very fast. We are all rowing together. Too bad you're not in our boat." That was not exactly where I was going with that lesson. But he then astutely observed, "You're only leaving to make one person happy, which is you. If you look at you, you don't look very happy." Out of the mouths of babes.

During the first raw weeks and months, I would start a countdown at about 5:00 P.M. How much longer until I could put them to bed? Would they notice that it was still light outside? When the last one was safely tucked in, I could then open the valve on my personal pressure cooker. After holding it together all day, I could finally release the carefully secured safety latch. Relief came in the form of tears, and plenty of them. On one evening, when I felt that the toll of the burden was indeed just too much for me to bear, I knelt by my bed and poured my heart out to the Lord. Another blessed and now familiar tender mercy followed: I felt the distinct physical impression of two hands on my shoulders. A touch was worth a thousand words. This experience unmistakably communicated to me, "You are not alone." I sobbed for several minutes at the thought of having this magnitude of heavenly support. I had *believed* I was not alone, but now I *knew;* and my testimony further grew.

For me, my anger was fairly short-lived. I had seen the tremendous disservice that anger had done to my own mother, and it wasn't something I cared to repeat. This singular event seemed to define her and cast the mold for her entire future. She would spend hours on the phone giving the unfortunate listener a detailed account about what a terrible person my dad was. "Wait a minute," I thought, "We share DNA with this person. What does that make us? Less than." It diminished us, and we felt less. From this, I resolved to avoid disparaging my children's father to them and, rather, focus on the positive parts that they could be proud of. Was it easy? No, but well worth the effort. And he has returned the favor, affording me the same respect.

Another delicate land mine in my parents' divorce was navigating the visits to my dad's home with his new wife. These forays were considered a betrayal. They were more like reconnaissance missions in enemy territory with intelligence reports expected upon our return. Occasionally, we would meet on neutral ground; but gradually the visits tapered off. After a couple of years, we mostly just exchanged birthday and Christmas cards. Not exactly a recipe for a relationship.

Although I'm sure that some anger has a healthy place in the grieving process, it doesn't take long for it to become counterproductive. At some point, it begs the question, "Do you want to live *in* this or *through* this?" After years of watching my mother simmer and stew in her own bitterness while my dad went on his way, living his life, it was clear that she was only hurting herself—and the children she meant to protect. As someone aptly described, "Anger is like a hot coal. If you hang onto it, you're the one who gets burned." Living through the unraveling of my own marriage, I preferred the adage, "Living well is the best revenge." I would not use my energy to dwell on things I could not change. I would *choose to be happy.* But first, there was a whole lot of sadness to get past.

I was mourning the death of a dream. I reasoned with myself that I didn't really want "him." Why would I want a person who cheated on me—when I was pregnant with his child, no less? I deserved better. I also philosophized that "if you aren't right for someone, by that very fact, they are not right for you." We all deserve to love and be loved. I just wanted him to be the person I wanted him to be. He wasn't.

Time to restructure. More coping mechanisms: I read, I prayed, I wrote. I poured my thoughts out on paper along with a cathartic tidal wave of tears, of which there seemed to be an unlimited supply. It provided a small but welcome respite. This nightly ritual was a small oasis in the desert of each long day. In addition to the listening ears of some very dear friends as well as my recently divorced sister, seeking comfort and wisdom from a higher source proved to be what truly gave me the strength to face another day. I kept telling myself that I just had to get through this day and then I could have a nervous breakdown tomorrow. The great thing about tomorrow is that it's always in the future, and so tomorrow never came.

One day my young son saw me crying in the laundry room. I had been so careful to spare the children. Should I tell him that I got some Clorox 2 in my eye or the truth? I knew I didn't want the kids to think that this was "no big deal" and that I wasn't ever sad. But, I also didn't want them to bear the weight of this. After a quick prayer in my heart, I settled on the truth. "Sometimes life just doesn't turn out the way that you plan, and right now I'm really sad that Dad doesn't live here, anymore."

"Oh, me too," he responded. "But, I love you, Mommy!"

At some point, my husband tried to tell me that our marriage had all been a lie and that he had never loved me. But my soul-searching had centered me. I would not continue to be buffeted by his beliefs when my own were just as valid. I told him that his experience had not been mine. I thought back to when I was supporting him through graduate school, when we were so poor that we could not even afford two bowls of clam chowder at Fisherman's Wharf. We had to share, but we could each have our own baguette, because they cost just 50 cents. So, for about three dollars, we could have "dinner and a show," sharing our soup while watching the street performers. I remembered doing all of the fun, silly things that two young newlyweds did in a big city. If it was free, we did it. My response to his assertion about our lack of a marriage was, "Well, do you know what? I was happy. And my perception is my reality. You can't take that away from me. I will remember those times as the good times that they were—for me." He seemed genuinely happy that I would be the keeper of a different history.

It's been ten years now, and on paper my life hasn't changed much. The kids have gotten older. And I'm still a divorced, single mother. But one thing I learned from my own absent father was that I did not want a Doorstep Dad for my kids. Mutually, we agreed that our love for our children hadn't changed, so we would put our differences aside and focus on cooperative parenting. We determined that we would rather share than divide the holidays and milestones with our children. After all, when I gave birth, it was not with "every other Christmas" in mind. Admittedly, this approach isn't the easiest; but when you go down this road, it's all hard. Still, the benefits of our post-divorce efforts have far outweighed the sacrifices. So for all of our sakes, I'm grateful that we've been able to put acrimony aside and put the children first. Through a conscious, constant effort, we have been able to create an unconventional sort of "fractured family," but one that works for us. The most important thing is that our children know they have two parents who no longer live under the same roof but who both love them very much.

For a long time, I used to think that my life was divided into B.C. and A.D.: before cheating and after divorce. But I refused to let this experience define me in a negative way. I am so much more than just a divorced person. At one point, I remember feeling like Scarlett O'Hara and saying to myself, "With God as my witness, this will not be the undoing of me." And sure enough, it wasn't. I'm not broken, and I don't need to be half of something else to be whole. Devastating as it was, I not only survived, but I learned and grew and became stronger in the process.

Yet another of the countless tender mercies that I received has become a sort of spiritual mantra for me. During one night of particular despair, after I had tucked the kids into bed, I was in the midst of my nightly devotional time of writing, praying, and reading when I began to pray for help more fervently than I ever had before. As I transitioned from this earnest prayer to my scripture reading, the page opened to Alma 31:31, 38:

> O Lord, my heart is exceedingly sorrowful; wilt thou comfort my soul in Christ. O Lord, wilt thou grant unto me that I may have strength, that I may suffer

with patience these afflictions which shall come upon me . . . And the Lord provided for them that they should hunger not, neither should they thirst; yea, and he also gave them strength, that they should suffer no manner of afflictions, save it were swallowed up in the joy of Christ. Now this was according to the prayer of Alma; and this because he prayed in faith.

I had heard about other people having the experience of their scriptures "falling open" to a certain, perfect passage, but now it had happened to me twice. *Me!* Was I even worthy to receive such mercy and such love? It was as if I had received direct and personal communication from Heavenly Father. It could not have felt more personal if a letter had arrived in my mailbox stamped "Heaven" in the return address corner.

The last verse did not say that we would suffer "no manner of afflictions." It said that we would suffer "no manner of afflictions *save it were swallowed up in the joy of Christ.*" I learned many things about the Atonement during this period of time in my life. I came to know that the Atonement did not just provide a compensation for sin, as I previously thought; its purpose is also to heal the effects of *all* pain and affliction, whatever the source. I felt this compensatory power regularly. It was almost as if the Lord were carrying me through this time of personal holocaust.

Years later, I asked the Lord in prayer why I didn't always feel the extent of comfort that I had felt earlier on. I was given to know that this was His way of telling me that I had grown and that I could handle more on my own at this point. What I now refer to as "The Analogy of the Shoelaces" came to my mind. If your three-year-old child came to you and asked for help tying her shoe, you would drop down on one knee and gladly offer to help. However, if your 13-year-old made a similar request, the inclination would be entirely different, knowing that the child could do it for herself. So now, when I feel that the help rendered is not as all-encompassing as it was in the beginning, I try to see it as a vote of confidence, reasoning, "The Lord must know that I can do this now." I have

learned to tie my own shoelaces. But surely, He will be there to
help me with my next obstacle in uncharted territory. I am grateful
for the knowledge I gained that we are truly never required to run
faster than we have strength.

Although I've been careful not to let the "Big D" define me,
there is no arguing that it has changed me. And I actually like the
person that I am now better than before. I wouldn't recommend this
makeover process to anyone, but I now have the gift of *knowing* the
truth of certain things as an indelible part of my testimony. I had
to get by on just *believing* before. When the scriptures say that "the
hairs on our head are numbered" and that "a sparrow doesn't fall
but what the Lord knows it," I now know this to be true. He knows
each one of us, individually, and is familiar with our own particular
Gethsemanes. He has traveled our paths so that he would better
know how to succor us. I know that the Atonement is real, the
Savior is indeed our elder brother, and His relationship with each
one of us is personal.

Without the strength I found in the Gospel of Jesus Christ,
I can't imagine having found the wherewithal to even get out of
bed in the morning, let alone carry on with my life. The Gospel
was and is quite literally my lifeline. In addition to the exponential
growth of my faith during this time, possibly one of the most
important things I learned was the value of perspective. I've learned
that although we can't always choose what happens in life, we can
always choose how we respond. By acting on a situation rather than
reacting, we do not let anyone control or dictate who we are. We
consciously choose, and therein lies our power. When we choose to
be grateful for what we have instead of angry for what we don't, we
empower ourselves to be happy. I choose to be happy. No matter
what happens, no one can take that away—a liberating thought.
After a decade of daily practice, our family has developed a strong
support system of "rowing together" toward a common goal. When
the seas get rough, faith serves as our sail, getting us farther than we
ever could on our own.

10

Little Red Hen

In the children's tale of the "Little Red Hen," a single mother from the barnyard finds a few grains of wheat while scratching in the yard for food for her family. As an industrious provider, Mother Hen decides to plant the wheat for a more abundant harvest instead of eating the few grains instantly. She asks for assistance from the other animals but gets no help from the duck, the pig, or the mouse. Mother Hen plants the wheat and watches it grow. With the help of her chicks, the Little Red Hen tends, waters, and cares for her crop. She harvests the ripe grain and threshes it without the help of the other animals. At last, she mills the grain and, with the flour, makes a delicious loaf of bread for her family.

Once the bread is baked, all the other animals are eager to enjoy the fruit of Mother Hen's labors. But Mother Hen refuses to share the bread with the animals who would not help to create the delicious loaf.

As a single mom, I admire Mother Hen's tenacity. She is persistent in working to achieve her goals and to create a provident living for her family. In the story, Mother Hen does not get angry with others' lack of support for her efforts. She does not flap her wings or peck at the self-centeredness of the other animals; instead, she continually invites them to join in the work at each phase of the project. Mother Hen cheerfully executes each step needed to make the bread, offering her chicks the healthy example of a strong work ethic and positive attitude—skills they will need in the future. Mother Hen understands the law of the harvest: we cannot reap the benefits when we do not do the required work or sowing. As Galatians 6:7 states, "Be not deceived; God is not mocked: for whatsoever a man soweth, that shall he also reap." So the unhelpful animals are not included in the feast of fresh bread.

There have been times when the needs of my children have left me feeling overwhelmed and inadequate. Like most of us, I turn to family, friends, associates, and ward members during times of need; and often my cup has been lovingly filled and my burdens lightened. But there are times in life when help is not forthcoming. Requests for assistance are declined or perhaps just not understood. In those times, I have felt tempted to stamp my feet or shake my fist at the obstacles that prevent me from nurturing my family according to the desires of my heart. How can I learn the patience of Mother Hen? How can I embody her quiet dignity and unwavering focus? Am I guilty of sounding like the barnyard animals when my own problems consume my attention to the point that I do not see the needs of others? Indeed, this classic tale offers me lessons well beyond those of my childhood understandings; lessons that lead to the source of all comfort, truth, and goodness. These are lessons that survive the test of time and, in my experience, even the test of divorce.

Shortly after my marriage ended, I struggled to secure health insurance for my children. Unsuccessful at every turn, I began to feel overwhelmed by gloom and dismay. Seeking comfort and strength, I sought a priesthood blessing from my home teacher. To my surprise, he responded with confusion at my request and a lack of empathy for my situation. Apparently unable to relate to my circumstances, he held up another single mother in our ward as a model of success and encouraged me to solve this issue on my own. I felt the painful sting of comparison and rejection. I was embarrassed and inclined toward anger. Reflecting on the wisdom of Mother Hen, however, I learned my first lesson:

Be gracious in the face of rejection,
and keep going.

With a softened heart, I let go of hard feelings and sought out another worthy priesthood holder who blessed me to be able to provide every needful thing for my family.

With three teenagers, two cars, and one working mom, transportation for our busy family was a juggling act. It was humbling for me to ask neighbors and ward members for help, but for one's children, a mother will ask nearly anything. I was particularly concerned about making sure my children could attend Seminary. With everything else they had been through, I did not want them to miss out on the spiritual reinforcement and fellowshipping they could receive there. While some friends were supportive and offered what they could, others were too busy. As one seminary teacher told me, getting rides for my children was "just too hard." As their mother, I am all too aware that my children's needs are primarily my responsibility, but I learned that despite my desire to be the mother who can "do it all," I couldn't. No one can. Everyone needs help. While Mother Hen did accomplish her task independent of help, who is to say what other important tasks did not get done that day because Mother Hen was left to do it all herself. Perhaps the chicks didn't get read to, or maybe somebody missed a piano lesson. The lesson I hadn't expected to learn from this experience was one meant for the barnyard animal in all of us. Knowing how difficult it was for me to ask for help in the first place, I realized that I was no different from anyone else. Asking for help is humbling. It can make us feel vulnerable. Most of us would not ask unless we truly needed it; and sooner or later, we all truly need another's help. My second lesson was clear:

Whenever possible, say "Yes!" By the time most people ask for help, you can be certain they need it.

None of us makes it through our trials alone, and divorce and single parenting is no exception. My times of need have taught me that when I hear the call to serve from others in need, I want to forsake the barnyard cry, "Not I!" and, instead, voice words that bring comfort and hope: "How can I help?"

This realization came with yet a third lesson, one the Savior taught often but one that can be easily forgotten in one's own hour of need:

Judge not.

I discovered that when my life was in chaos, my empathy for others was limited. My own pain overwhelmed me, so I allowed myself to believe that others in my life were enjoying an easier existence without the degree of struggle and pain I was experiencing. I came close to resenting them for the ease of their lives as well as for their inability to reach out to me. Fortunately, I soon realized that those who seemed unsympathetic to my needs had unseen sorrows of their own that surely clouded their ability to feel empathy for my challenges. They needed my love and support as much as I needed theirs.

In another well-known parable, the Savior spoke of a man traveling from Jerusalem to Jericho who fell among thieves and was left naked, wounded, and half-dead on the road. Many of our trials have a similar emotional effect. During my divorce, I felt broken and injured. I felt hurt, alone, and desperate for care. As with the Priest and Levite in the parable, there were times when well-intentioned people were unable to assist me, largely because their life experiences had not developed in them empathy for my type of loss. But some friends saw and understood my pain. Some of my personal Good Samaritans had overcome experiences akin to mine and knew how to soothe and comfort me; others just knew how to listen and love.

After nearly 23 years of marriage, the life I had known changed drastically. Divorce brought with it the need to move out of the home I loved and into a rental home I most certainly did not love. Sadness and shock overwhelmed me. To allay my depression and angst, I began a regimen of walking every day. My first excursion was only two or three blocks; that was all it took before a friend appeared and walked by my side. From then on, she walked with me and talked with me for as long as I needed, whenever I needed. She and her patient husband became my Good Samaritans as they listened to my fears, nursed my wounds, and bandaged my broken heart.

My final lesson emerged from the whole of my experience, teaching me how to not just survive, but how let my spirit thrive:

Be grateful, no matter what.

Developing gratitude empowered me as I healed. As I found thank you notes to write and blessings to acknowledge, I felt more aware of the goodness in my life and felt greater empathy for others and their struggles. Finding beauty on my walks, listening to uplifting music, reading scriptures, giving service, and participating in enjoyable activities filled my heart with joy and peace. During the most difficult times, I developed an appreciation for the gifts of empathy and charity as demonstrated by our Savior, Jesus Christ. He truly knows our pains and knows how to heal us.

While teaching the gospel to the people of Gideon, Alma described the infinite empathy of our Savior.

> And he shall go forth, suffering pains and afflictions and temptations of every kind; and this that the work might be fulfilled which saith he will take upon him the pains and the sicknesses of his people. And he will take upon him death that he may loose the bands of death which bind his people; and he will take upon him their infirmities, that his bowels may be filled with mercy, according to the flesh, that he may know according to the flesh how to succor his people according to their infirmities. (Alma 7:11–12)

Our Savior Jesus Christ understands and is our source of mercy and hope.

When we use our sorrows to develop empathy for others we emulate our Savior. When we are patient with people who have good intentions but cannot understand what we suffer, we follow in our Savior's example of forgiveness. When I reach out for support and am met with the barnyard cry, "Not I," I think of the Little Red Hen and keep striving with patience and hope without letting the opinions of others slow down my progress. When I remember that many souls around me are injured in ways I don't understand, I can offer a gracious reply that may soften their hearts and ease their burdens.

I have learned the value of making meaningful connections with the people I am blessed to have in my life. And I enjoy with gratitude the sweet blessings of my life and the opportunity to grow, even from my challenges. For surely, as with the Little Red Hen, when we do these things, our bread will be delicious.

11

Finding Good Fruit

It was Sunday morning, and the clock radio prodded me to get the day going. The sun was shining through the dingy blinds of my small bedroom window in the house I had rented for myself and my three teenagers. I pulled back the quilt my mother made for me, my one physical comfort in our depressing surroundings, and swung my feet over the side of the bed to put on my slippers. I would never allow my bare feet to touch the original orange shag carpet in this old, neglected house.

I walked down the hall to the master bedroom shared by Karl, age 19, and his thirteen-year-old younger brother, Frank, to tell them it was time to get ready for church. Although Karl had forfeited having his own room when we moved to this house, he did not complain; and, Frank was comforted by having his big brother near him. The master bedroom had a terrible smell, and I had not scrubbed the adjoining bathroom with bleach, yet. The windows in this room looked out over an unkempt backyard with unpruned trees dropping neglected and rotting pieces of fruit.

Carly, my fifteen-year-old daughter, finished in the shower in the hall bathroom and returned to her room. She handled our sudden move more graciously than I had expected for a girl her age. Carly had relinquished her lovely lavender bedroom with sheer white curtained windows overlooking our previous charming neighborhood. Now the view through her grimy bedroom window showed waist-high weeds among abandoned red landscaping rock with broken chunks of cement and pieces of fence. This had not been an easy transition for my children, but they rose to the occasion.

After losing my temple marriage of 23 years and my dream house, I looked forward to going to church not only for the social support but for the spiritual strength my children and I desperately needed. At times the lessons were difficult to hear through a broken heart, but I went anyway, searching for the sweet peace and comfort we needed in our uprooted lives.

During one particular Relief Society lesson, we were studying the principles of developing faith as laid out in Alma chapter 32 of the Book of Mormon. The verses were familiar and enlightening until we read the last sentence in verse 43: "Then, my brethren, ye shall reap the rewards of your faith, and your diligence, and patience, and long-suffering, waiting for the tree to bring forth fruit unto you." When I read this scripture, something snapped in my chest, like the wind had been knocked out of my lungs. One thought haunted me: For 23 years I had been faithful, diligent, patient and longsuffering in my marriage; and despite my efforts, I had only received bad fruit in return.

Tears welled up in my eyes as I made my escape from the lesson, collected my children, and drove home to our unattractive rental home. I quickly changed my clothes, walked to the backyard, and stared down the ugly fruit on the bothersome citrus tree. The pieces of fruit falling from the tangled tree were twice the size of an average grapefruit with green, stippled skins and very thick rinds. I could not think of a good use for the fruit and resented the rotting mounds covering the yard. I promptly decided that the bad fruit had to be discarded immediately. With a ladder, pruning shears, and a rake, I attacked that wild and neglected tree, pulled down the strange, large, round fruit and raked up the decaying balls of citrus.

As I was balanced atop the ladder, my visiting teacher came into the backyard, her eyes wide in amazement at the sight of me unapologetically hacking down overgrown branches. I explained my sudden and irresistible need to remove this ugly fruit from my yard that day. Like the good visiting teacher she was, she listened as I sobbed and complained that I did not have any good fruit in my life. She comforted me and showed me love and support. In that moment of despair, she assured me that the Lord had not and would not abandon me.

Time passed, and my wounded heart began to heal. As it did, my eyes were opened to many sweet blessings that poured in for my children and me. Life became enjoyable again. I loved being with my children. I soaked in the beauty of nature. I walked and talked with dear friends. Karl went on a mission. Carly's boyfriend joined the Church. Frank developed more confidence and improved his grades in school. And finally, the miracle I had been waiting for came when I was able to buy a beautiful new home just a few blocks from the rental house.

When Karl returned from serving his mission in Canada, he returned to a lovely home and a bedroom of his own. I accompanied Karl as he reported on his mission to the stake High Council. After Karl's report, I shared my testimony and my heartfelt love of the Lord and His gospel. The highlight for me came when I told the brethren that after exercising much faith, diligence, patience and long-suffering, I now tasted the good fruit described in the scriptures.

One day, I was browsing in the produce department of a grocery store. In the citrus section I found a display advertising pummelos for $2.49 a pound. To my surprise, pummelos were a large round citrus fruit with thick rinds. They looked just like the strange fruit I detested so much in the backyard of our rented house. I later learned that pummelos are the largest of the citrus fruits and are native to Southeast Asia. Pummelos or Pomelos arrived in China around 100–200 B.C. and are given as presents

during Chinese New Year celebrations as a symbol of good fortune
and prosperity. Pomelos are a popular choice for breakfast, salads,
and exotic entrees.

The irony was not lost on me. I had had good fruit all
along but could not see it through my sorrow and self pity. I
have learned that during challenging times you may have to look
harder to see the blessings. But they are still there, often right in
our own backyards. I now know to look for beauty and joy, even
if it is hidden under thick rinds and tangled branches. I strive to
remember what our Savior taught us about finding good fruit from
our Father in Heaven:

> Or what man is there of you, whom if his son ask
> bread, will he give him a stone? Or if he ask a fish, will
> he give him a serpent? If ye then, being evil, know how
> to give good gifts unto your children, how much more
> shall your Father which is in heaven give good things
> to them that ask him? (Matthew 7:9–11)

I have tasted the fruit, and it is delicious.

12

The Blessing of Duct Tape

Through all the changes, twists, and turns in my life, staying firm in my faith has proven to be the anchor that helps me weather life's unpredictable storms. So it has been through the trauma of leaving my marriage of 23 years. Our church encourages good functioning families, ideally with both mother and father to care for and rear children. While I do not disagree, I sometimes sit amidst my congregation and can't help but feel unlike the admirable intact families around me.

One Sunday as I watched the young Priests replace the white cloth over the Sacrament table, I thought about what I would bring to God's altar if an account of my stewardship were required. Sorrow filled my heart as I visualized myself reporting on my broken and fractured family. Had I done everything possible to prevent this disaster? How could such a failure be reconciled? What would the Lord want from me now?

A memory came to mind of a seventh grade science project that I had helped my daughter with a few years before. Caitlin's assignment was to create a machine able to lift a fifteen-ounce can. The project was exasperating. I went with Caitlin to turn in the assigned machine. We carried it into the classroom on a wood board and presented it to the teacher for inspection. The science teacher was very experienced and had surely seen many projects during his years in the classroom. He appeared unimpressed but acknowledged the project had been submitted on time.

Another student brought in a machine that brought a giant smile to the teacher's face. This young man's project was received warmly by the excited teacher, and his solid-looking machine was anxiously inspected. The teacher rubbed his hands together with anticipation as the student pulled the lever to demonstrate how it lifted the can; and, calculations were made measuring the effectiveness of the machine. The machine did perform the required work and showed marginal effectiveness. The teacher smiled at the young student.

A third student pulled a machine out of her backpack. She had carried her project on her back the entire school day. Her machine was made of disjointed tubes of PVC pipe and appeared to be too flimsy to lift the can as required. The girl assembled her machine on the lab table, but some of the PVC pipe would not connect as she had expected. The teacher shook his head, frowned slightly, and went behind his desk to get a roll of duct tape. He wrapped the duct tape where the machine needed reinforcement until the connections held tight and the experiment could proceed. We were all surprised when the unsteady machine was able to lift the can off the lab table easily. When calculations were made, the effectiveness of the flimsy duct-tape-reinforced machine was superior to the first, more solid-looking machine. The teacher scratched his head and marked his grade book.

Like the flimsy machine, I had been bounced around by life's experiences and did not feel capable of lifting the load assigned to me. I too needed duct tape to help fortify my best efforts. While my friends and family did not always understand the extent of my sorrow, they offered support where they could. Others I had met with similar challenges offered listening ears and empathy that soothed my soul. I also discovered that when I searched for ways to help others, I found support for my own struggles.

Fortunately, we are not left alone to fix our lives. To believe so is a form of pride that limits us from reaching out to others and to our Heavenly Father. The only constant source for our "duct tape" fortifications is our Savior, Jesus Christ.

I take comfort in knowing that my weaknesses and failings will not disqualify me from the benefits of the Lord's healing as long as I try my best. I no longer hold myself responsible for others' mistakes or hold myself to others' standards of what they can accomplish. I know now that my path, imperfect as it may be, is my own to forge. Flimsy as I may sometimes feel, with the reinforcing help of my Heavenly Father and Savior, I can pick up all the cans I have been assigned—and make something of them, too.

13

My Alaska Misadventure

In June of 1995, I was living in Kodiak, Alaska with my husband, who was a police officer. Before that, we had lived on a small island in the village of Ouzinkie. While he was away for training in Anchorage, my husband called me at home after having been to a late movie, reportedly alone. He said he'd like to stay away longer to have a golf weekend with some guys from work. None of it sounded right. I told myself it was nothing, but the sleepless night that followed indicated that I knew it was something, and something big.

Sure enough, when my husband returned from that trip, he came with a prepared message: He loved me but wasn't in love with me, anymore. Shock and numbness are all I remember. I asked the usual battery of questions. Why? When? Was there someone else?

"Don't be silly," he said, apparently to reassure me. But most of my self-assurance evaporated when I learned that he had felt this way for some time. Where was I amidst this important development? Why was this the first I had heard about the unraveling of my marriage? It seemed so unfair. I didn't sleep at all that night.

Thankfully, my family was coming for a visit in two weeks. Although this news was sure to ruin their visit, I needed them. I called my sister Marilyn the next morning and was lovingly assured that my family would be there to help me through this. My boss understood my distress and gave me some needed time off of work. The only one seemingly undisturbed by this tumultuous revelation was my husband. The next day he went to work as usual and came home acting as if nothing had happened. He was still looking forward to the upcoming fishing trip with my family and seemed strangely content. I felt a lot of things that week; but most of all, I was utterly confused.

I attempted to normalize my life by going back to work and trying to resume my normal routine, but I felt numb. I didn't eat or sleep much. I probably looked like a zombie. Before long, my husband planned a trip to our former town of Ouzinkie, supposedly to stay with some of our friends and think things over. The idea of time alone to think appealed to me as well, so I agreed this could be good for us.

To the contrary, it turned out to be a long and lonely weekend. I tried to act happy at church, but the Relief Society lesson centered on husbands and the priesthood. I couldn't help noting the stark contrast between the noble examples held up in the lesson and the husband who I feared was about to abandon me.

My husband came home from his weekend away more distant than ever. He wouldn't talk about our marriage or his feelings for me. On some level I probably knew what that meant, but by the next day it was all laid out for me by a dear friend who knew more than I did. As it turned out, my husband was having a relationship with the daughter of our friends with whom he had been staying in Ouzinkie. I did the necessary follow-up to confirm the truth of my friend's claim. Sure enough, it was true. I confronted my husband with my discovery, but there was little left to say. He couldn't deny it or make it better, nor did he want to. I had left my home and family and come all the way to Alaska for my husband. Now here I was, rejected and alone. I was devastated.

I didn't know how I would make it through each day after that. I felt profound loss and desperately lost. But I also felt the unconditional love and support of family and God. Even though they were far away, my family cried with me, comforted me, and gave me hope for a brighter tomorrow. When I thought nothing would ever be okay again, my mom helped me believe it would be. My family went ahead with the trip to Alaska; but instead of coming to visit and sightsee, they came to take me home. I left almost everything behind and left Alaska with almost nothing: no husband, no home, no children, and what felt like no dignity. I was humiliated. I felt like I was living a nightmare and kept hoping I would wake up and find that none of it was real. But nothing could feel more real than the pain of boarding that plane and saying goodbye to the husband and life I loved.

The only thing that kept me going was the help of my Father in Heaven and our Lord, Jesus Christ. I prayed every five minutes to give me the strength to make it through each day and to know I would be all right. Even when I was out at restaurants or movies, I would have to excuse myself to go to the restroom to pray that I wouldn't fall apart.

The Lord did hold me together, although it got worse before it got better. One month after my exodus from Alaska, my husband informed me that he and his girlfriend were expecting a baby together. The fact that I hadn't been able to have children made that especially painful to hear. The phrase, "Life isn't fair" took on a new meaning for me. But I survived. I absorbed each new blow as it came. There was no secret to my survival. I just kept going. Every day was a struggle; and at the end of each day, I would congratulate myself for simply surviving another day. Eventually I survived many days, each one day at a time. And with the support of my family and the Lord, I actually started to feel better. Every day got easier.

I went back to work with my family at their courier service and, through our business, met a wonderful man who was also divorced and had a four-year-old daughter. Five months later, we were married! We have now been married for thirteen years; and in addition to our now eighteen-year-old beautiful daughter, we have a wonderful eleven-year-old son. I finally got the husband of my dreams and the children I had prayed for.

I have always heard, "When the Lord closes a door, He opens a window," and He really did! I could not have made it through this most difficult time in my life without the help and love of the Lord. He gave me the strength to continue on when all I wanted to do was curl up into a ball and melt away. I would not have believed it at the time, but this trial strengthened me as a person as well as my testimony of my loving Heavenly Father. I came to realize how much I love the Lord, and I saw firsthand how much He loves me. I know now that His suffering allowed Him to help me through my heartache. Leaning on His love and strength, I made it through!

14

You Make Me Feel Like Dancin'

Dating after divorce is not for the faint of heart. It is an interesting experience to find yourself single and seeking companionship in the middle or later years of life, especially if this is not your first time down this road. In my post-divorce experience, I have found that some things about dating have changed from my first go-around, while others have stayed (sometimes regrettably), the same. I have had my share of novel, surprising, and awkward experiences as I have gotten myself back into the dating game. And despite the fact that they are not my most "successful" courting experiences, I think there is benefit to sharing them. I certainly don't wish to add fuel to your own fears and hesitations about dating after divorce (if you have them), and I likewise would never want to sound like I am poking fun at the people I have met along my journey. Like me, I know they are doing the best they can in their own circumstances. Instead, I share them because, for most of us, they are an inevitable part of the (sometimes trying) process of finding love again later in life. And while uncomfortable and even discouraging in the moment, these haphazard experiences have a way of ripening into sweet memories that bring a smile and remind me not to take myself (and others) too seriously.

As a devoted LDS woman who also happens to be divorced with children, dating has proved to be difficult for me. Setting aside the challenge of finding a lifetime or eternal partner, I have found that just going on a simple date, the kind I went on back in college, can be a significant task.

My divorced friends have not been all that encouraging. Their comments range from, "Forget it, there is no one out there," to "Remember what it was like going to dances when we were teenagers? Nothing has changed!" They did not fill me with hope about this process. Still, I did not want to believe them. I convinced myself that by virtue of being older and wiser, this would be a piece of cake. After all, I had survived a difficult divorce and was successfully raising four children, fulfilling church callings, working full time, and doing community service. How hard could dating be?

As it turns out, it can be pretty hard. For starters, many things that had changed since I was single the first time around, like the way you meet people and get a date. After my divorce, I decided to attend an LDS single adult conference with another divorced mom I knew. (Side note: Always take a friend along when you're about to go way out of your comfort zone!) Some naysayers had told me that going to a singles conference would be a waste of time, but I chose not to believe them. The theme of the conference was based on a quote by President Spencer W. Kimball, the prophet of my teenage years: "We have paused on some plateaus long enough. Let us resume our journey forward and upward." I had paused long enough on my plateau and was ready to move on. I felt prompted to put aside my fears and begin to reach out of the protective shell I had built around myself and my children. And I was glad I did. The conference was fun, and the workshops especially were amazing. The speakers were funny and inspiring, and the content was so relevant to our LDS, divorced lifestyles. That part of the conference was great. It was the social aspect for which I was utterly unprepared.

Among my first new "single experiments" was participating in the latest trend called "speed dating." According to the rules of speed dating, I would meet sixteen men my age, talk to them one-on-one for a few minutes, then move on to the next person with no obligation or future commitment. I am all about streamlining and multitasking, so sixteen dates in one evening sounded perfect to me!

The first gentleman sitting across from me was attractive and seemed nice. The facilitator blew the whistle to begin, and we were on our way.

"Hello, I have never done this before," I said. "Do you have a question you want to ask me to get this conversation started?"

He responded simply, "Yes, do you want to move to Canada?"

Wow, that's an unusual question, I mused. I was expecting something more along the lines of, "Do you live in the area?" or "Have you been single long?" or "Do you like chocolate?" Something I could answer relatively easily without committing to a life-changing move.

"No, I have never wanted to move to Canada. Are you from there?" I said lightly, just in case he was kidding around and I missed the joke.

"Yes, I am looking for a wife to move back to Canada with me," he said. I had to give the man credit. Not only did he get straight to the point, but he threw in some international travel with the deal!

"Would you be interested?" he continued.

"No thanks, I am staying here in California," I said and gestured toward my seat. The silence that followed seem to stretch for hours. Where was the woman with the whistle to move us on to our next date?

Three long minutes finally passed, and the whistle blew. On to the next gentleman.

"Do you have any animals?" he opened.

"No, I have four children. I don't need another mess to clean up," I said with a smile.

"Oh, that's too bad," he said. "My little Buttercup gives me such joy and pleasure. I come home from work every night, and she is there to greet me. We play in the park, chase butterflies, and run through blades of grass together. It is the best part of my day."

"Wow, that is great that you love your dog so much," I replied.

"I'm talking about my cat!" he corrected enthusiastically.

I couldn't think of a single response. Once again, we sat in silence. Did that monitor woman leave the room? Help! What do I say next? Finally, two and a half long minutes later, the whistle blew. So far I had found my two least compatible matches in the room. It had to get better!

The third gentleman to sit across from me looked promising. "What is your profession?" I asked, hopeful.

"Comedy," he answered.

Yes! I thought. *Now we are getting somewhere.* I love funny people, and I love to laugh. "Do you have a routine you use?" I asked eagerly.

"What, you want me to tell you a joke?"

"Sure, I would love that," I said enthused.

"Okay," he said, "Now pay attention. If I take this orange and throw it at the trash can and it bounces out, I have two options. I can either go over to it, pick it up and put it in the can, or I can pick it up and walk out the door." He paused.

"Okay," I said, waiting to hear the remainder of the joke.

"That's it. Didn't you get it?" he asked, stunned.

"No, I didn't get it."

"Well you must not be up-to-date on your humor," he retorted.

Unsure of how any development in the comedy world could make that funny, I nodded my head and said as sweetly as I could, "You better keep your day job."

Whistle please! Someone out there better whistle.

I didn't hold out much hope for my fourth "date," but he sat down quickly and started right in. "Hello, my name is Juan. I live in a two-bedroom apartment, I am 5'4," and I weigh 140 pounds."

I answered in turn, "Hello Juan, my name is Laie. I live in a three-bedroom house. I am 5'6," and I am not telling you how much I weigh," I quipped pleasantly back, sure that I had charmed him with my clever reply.

He came back, "Hello, my name is Juan. I live in a two-bedroom apartment, I am 5'4," and I weigh 140 pounds."

Realizing we may have a language barrier to bridge, I said slowly, "Hello Juan, it's very nice to meet you." Juan once again replied,

"Hello, my name is Juan. I live in a two-bedroom apartment, I am 5'4," and I weigh 140 pounds."

I felt like I was in a scene from *The Princess Bride*, in which the character Inigo Montoya introduces himself over and over using the same prescripted lines. It at least brought a smile to my face as I replayed that scene in my head and waited again for three long minutes to pass.

Seventeen potential suitors later, I had failed to make a connection with any. *Oh well, you can't win them all,* I thought. So I decided to try a singles dance.

I knew the single adult conference would be hosting a dance, and I was excited to meet new people and get myself out on the dance floor after all these years. But despite my willing attitude and cute strappy sandals, the first hour passed without getting asked to dance even once. I decided to take matters into my own hands and asked a seemingly nice man to dance. To my surprise his response was an unapologetic "No." Hmmm. Okay. Rejection—to my face and right off the bat. I wasn't expecting that, but I didn't let it stop me from trying. I got back on the proverbial horse and asked another man to dance. Strangely enough, he turned me down as well! Now I was getting a complex. I ran to the bathroom to check my teeth, face, hair, anything that might be wrong with me. Everything was in place, so back to the dance floor I went, but with only enough confidence to ask my girlfriend to go out and dance with me. Fortunately, *she* did not turn me down!

My second experience at a singles dance was even more lively. One night, closer to home, a divorced friend and I decided to take a chance on a church singles dance in our area. How wrong could we go for four dollars? We came fashionably late, remembering that to be the norm, but still found that the dance hadn't quite gotten off the ground, yet. To be precise, there were five people sitting at tables and no one on the dance floor! We decided to go for ice cream and give the party a chance to get going. Not much had changed upon our return, so my friend and I decided that instead of waiting to be asked, we'd get out on the floor with each other and start dancing. The music was unfamiliar and hard to dance to. We found ourselves bouncing up and down and pumping our arms for lack of any other moves that seemed to fit the music. I realize it can be hard to find appropriate music these days, but we wondered if there weren't something out there with good lyrics that didn't leave us looking like tribal dancers.

Nevertheless, the ritual soon worked for my friend, and she got asked to dance by a 6'7" tall gentleman. He looked especially large next to my friend but since it was a fast dance they fared okay. I watched diligently for the girlfriend rescue signal: for us, scratching your nose means "get me out of here"; fluffing your hair means, "he's kinda cute"; and running from the room—well, I don't need to explain that one.

There I stood alone, watching for the cue and trying to keep beat with the music, when I finally got approached by a man.

"Do you ballroom dance?" he asked.

Despite my significant height advantage and his crooked toupee, I thought it wasn't a bad opening line. I answered honestly that I didn't know how to ballroom dance but left it open for a variety of follow-up options.

He continued, "Do you dance at all?"

Given that I had been dancing when he approached me, I didn't know whether or not to take offense. So I said with a big smile, "Well, I sort of dance. See, I just go like this," and proceeded to move my shoulders and arms around a little bit. I thought I was being cute; but judging from his next move, his inquiry was apparently motivated by a different goal than getting to know me. He pulled his wallet from his back pocket and handed me a business card. "If you want to know how to ballroom dance, I can teach you." Then he walked away, leaving me alone on the sidelines, holding his card as a token of my dancing inability.

At this point I really started wondering if there might be something wrong with me. I am attractive, I was smiling, and I have all of my teeth and hair. What was the deal?! When my friend returned from her dance, I was determined to get myself out on that dance floor, even if I had to ask someone, myself. My friend had already secured two dances with the tall gentleman, and here I was having to do this the hard way. But I was determined. I surveyed the room for an unsuspecting prospect, when I felt a tap on my shoulder.

"You want to dance?" I heard from behind.

Yes! Now things were starting to look up. I darted toward the dance floor with him in tow before he had a chance to hand me his business card and walk away like the last guy.

I smiled as we danced, and he asked my name. I said something that must have sounded like ". . . arry."

"Terry?" he asked.

I repeated, ". . . arry."

"Oh, Mary?"

I nodded my head, content that my name for this dance would be Mary. Oddly, had we not been at a dance I would have sworn this man was on his way to a pool or the beach. Trying not to stare, but I couldn't help but notice that he was wearing swimming goggles. Honest-to-goodness swimming goggles. I was intrigued, to say the least.

"Do you live close by here?" I asked, suddenly wanting to know more about this curious fellow.

"No, I haven't had hair for a long time," he answered, smiling.

"Oh." I nodded in agreement. He was indeed bald, although I had not intended to make that a point of conversation.

He went on, "I wish we could keep in touch with people we meet at the dances through email." I nodded and smiled thinking how grateful I was for just the opposite. When the dance ended, I thanked him politely, turned to my girlfriend, and proceeded to pull my nose practically off my face—the "get me out of here" sign times twenty. Deciding we'd ventured out of our comfort zone enough for one night, we ran to the car and sped away, laughing hysterically as my girlfriend tossed the business card for my future dancing lessons out the window. What a night!

Fortunately, dances and speed dating are not the only ways to meet people when you're single. But I don't believe these experiences were a failure. I now know that it is not easy to find a man I want to share my life with, but for now the important thing is that I keep myself open to that possibility. I have decided to be proactive in my desire to remarry. I am willing to take a few chances to meet people, and I won't let myself hide behind the excuse that I am shy. I tell myself this is not the hardest thing I have ever done. And I know that if I turn to the Lord in prayer, he will direct me.

Being a divorced LDS mother has allowed me to learn patience and long-suffering in a different way than even my marriage taught me. And I am still learning. I feel my Savior's love and his healing hand on my heart helping me to be willing to trust again and have fun again.

I have made the decision to keep smiling and keep dancing. Both my friend and I have since found wonderful men to date through an online site. That may not work for everyone, but it turned out great for us. I know that dances and conferences and speed dating and online dating services may or may not be the means to making a lasting connection with someone; but I have little to lose and a lot of good experiences (and occasionally, good laughs) to gain.

For me, this is all part of rebuilding life after divorce. Even after the tragic turn my life took after 17 years of marriage, I can heal and grow and try new things. With a positive and grateful attitude and a reliance on the Lord's strength, I can start anew.

I believe anyone can have a second chance at love and companionship if you are willing to risk a little and trust again. I know the Lord knows our fears and heartaches and can heal our hearts. For our part, we just have to be willing to get out on the floor and dance again!

15

The Only Way Out Is Through

My Dad used to say, "Sometimes the only way out is through." I have taken that philosophy to heart, and it has seen me *through* many a hard time. Getting through the pain of my divorce was preceded by getting through the pains of a very difficult marriage. In fact, about sixteen and a half years of my seventeen-year marriage were spent in serious struggle. Still, I never imagined the words "I am filing for divorce" would ever leave my mouth.

I was raised in an active LDS family with parents whose temple marriage has been blessing our family for 49 years now. The word "divorce" was not in my vocabulary growing up. The divorced people I knew all had fidelity issues, so I thought barring that I would be safe from anything that could destroy my marriage. Sadly, our marriage was never a team effort, and my husband was not interested in loving, providing, and protecting our family. I held on and fought for our family for 17 years, until I knew there was nothing more I could do. I surrendered to the truth and let him go.

I guess it should make me feel better that somewhere around half of the population, in and out of the church, has either spoken or heard those words. But it doesn't. As most who are divorced know, it is something you would not wish on your worst enemy. Sitting in a courtroom across from the person to whom you once said "I do" is not a happy place to be. It leads an otherwise sane person to ponder and question many things: your perception of reality for one, the security of your future for another. The question I kept asking myself was, "Is there life after divorce?" Marriage was all I had known for nearly two decades. Going through life as a single person seemed frightening and intimidating. I tried to assure myself that, of course, life would go on after divorce. I likened it to a mother asking if there was life after childbirth. The travails of childbirth can be painful and frightening, but it is a means to a new beginning. Having given birth to four children and having lived to tell the tale, I had hope that this too would pass.

What my life would look like after divorce was a different question, one I am still finding answers to. In fact, this new phase of my life is full of unanswered questions; but they are ones I now feel ready to face on my own, with the Lord's help. I am alone, and sometimes it is a lonely place to be. But I pray for strength and peace every day; and I know the Lord, who also suffered loneliness, knows how to comfort me. I believe the Lord blesses us for doing our best through our earthly trials. I know my Savior loves me because of the peace and hope that only He could bring into my heart and mind.

Divorce is painful in every way: emotionally, physically, spiritually, and financially. Going through it alone is even more painful. But sometimes severing an abusive or destructive relationship is necessary. Having a loving Heavenly Father makes the healing process much easier. When I reach up, he is there; and if ever I don't feel Him there, it is not because He has pulled back. It is because I neglected to reach up.

"Why me?" is a question many of us ask in reaction to difficult trials. I know it is best not to dwell on that question, but sometimes I take a moment to ponder the "what" and "why" in hope that I can learn from my trials. Like everyone, I have shortcomings and lessons to learn. I am not immune from making mistakes and needing the Refiner's fire. But I love to give of myself and help others; and if anything, this experience has given me more compassion and empathy for others hurting like I have. I hope I can be an instrument in helping others come through their refiner's fire because of the things I have learned.

How to make it *through* is a question I take one day at a time. Letting myself experience the myriad of emotions helps, even when they come all at once (typically resulting in a puzzled expression on my face, an enormous hiccup, and a mixture of laughter and tears). Some emotions I simply pass through, and some emotions pass through me—sometimes like a torrent. When emotion overwhelms me, I fall to my knees in sobs and pray for protection around my heart. I survived many difficult years of marital pain this way; and as surely as the Lord was there for me then, he is here for me now.

I have heard about tender mercies all my life. I believe in them. I look for them. When I find them, I focus on those blessings. When they don't come quickly, I wait and hope that tomorrow will be better.

Divorce can't be explained by any one person or any one person's story. Every person's experience is unique, but we all have to get from one side of the experience to the other. How we get *through* is up to us. I made it through by leaning on the Lord. He was the protector of my heart and home and family. He has lightened my burdens and healed my soul. He sees me through, as I know He will for you.

16

New Hopes, New Dreams

Divorce. Like everything else in life, we truly don't know the emotional, physical, and mental impact of something until we are in the midst of it, ourselves. The old adage of not judging someone until you've walked in her shoes is so very true. I had been married for 23 years with four children, ages 16–21, at the time my husband moved out. Only the youngest was still living at home. My husband and I had been living his dream of building our own home on two acres in the woods. We had agreed that I could go back to school and fulfill my dream of finishing my education when the house was complete. We lived in the home just one year when I began working on my bachelor's degree. One month after I started school, my husband moved out.

Besides feeling shorted on our agreement, I felt broken-hearted and profoundly rejected from the person who knew me and, I thought, loved me better than anyone else. The person with whom I had trusted my life didn't want me, anymore. My hopes were crushed along with my self-esteem. Shortly after my husband moved out and moved on with someone else, I lamented to my son about the sorrows of feeling so easily replaceable. My son's response took me by surprise. "Mom, we're all replaceable." Depressing as it sounded, in a sense he was right. Life keeps going on with or without us, whether or not our world is spinning as we'd like it to.

On the outside, I felt like Humpty Dumpty, broken and in pieces with no one to put me back together again. But inside, I knew that wasn't true. With God's help, I could put myself and my life back together again and move forward.

Divorce wasn't what I wanted, but that didn't seem to matter. The drama leading to the breakdown of our marriage is not important to recount here as much as what I learned about surviving the unexpected. Divorce changed my world dramatically in every way; but most of all, it forced me to change my dreams. From as long as I can remember, being a wife and a mother have been my dreams and life's ambition. Losing that dream was incredibly hard to let go of. Thankfully, I still had my children; but our family was forever changed, fragmented. It felt at odds with my spiritual ideal of a forever family. I suppose it doesn't matter what your dream is; when dreams are shattered for whatever reason, it is devastating. The anxiety I felt from my sudden and extreme aloneness was overwhelming. This was supposed to be the time my husband and I enjoyed together—traveling and having fun after raising our children. At least one of us was enjoying the fruits of our labors; but he was with someone other than me. I was, instead, left with a life that was a blank slate of which I had no idea how to fill.

For the first while I didn't sleep at night, and I couldn't concentrate during the day. I often sat at my computer at work and cried. I debated dropping out of school, because I struggled to focus and keep up with the homework. After many hours in prayer trying to figure out what direction to go, I realized that going to college gave me something productive to focus my attention on. I was working towards my bachelor's degree in Psychology, which worked to my advantage because so much of my studies overlapped with issues my kids and I were dealing with. Besides preparing me for a better career, school ended up being very therapeutic. The topics I have studied have helped me understand my own experiences better; and in turn, my experiences have brought a depth and understanding to the things I study. Because writing has been so integral to my healing process, I chose to study the power of writing in healing from trauma. I have been blessed to see the bigger picture of how my struggles are part of a larger lesson that is the human experience.

A big part of the lesson for me has been learning to accept change. We lived in a very small town, which has its benefits but can, at times, feel like living under a microscope. I wanted to move, but moving terrified me. Where would I go? What would I do? How would I support myself? What would my new life be like for my kids? I had always had a strong faith in God; but between the grief of my present and the fear of my future, even my faith was shaken. These words by Marilyn Ferguson describe just how I felt:

> It's not so much that we're afraid of change or so in love with the old ways, but it's that place in between that we fear . . . It's like being between trapezes. It's Linus when his blanket is in the dryer. There's nothing to hold on to.

I wrestled and questioned for a good while but eventually grabbed onto my faith tighter than ever. In the end, I realized there was nothing else to hold on to, nothing of any real strength or solace. God became, quite literally, my constant companion and confidant.

The healing process is different for everyone; for me, the first year after my husband left was the hardest. My life hung in limbo, and I struggled to just hold on to what balance and order I had. Fortunately, I had wonderful girlfriends who carried me through. Girls' night became an escape and reprieve from our troubles. We cooked, ate, and, most importantly, laughed a lot. No matter how depressing my situation became, my girlfriends helped me find humor in the absurdities of life.

I surrounded myself with positive, uplifting people and activities to keep me from drowning in my sorrows. I started my mornings off with prayer and scriptures to give me peace, and yoga to relieve my anxiety. I joined a triathlon training class that got me in shape, kept me busy, and surrounded me with outgoing people. I also listened to media that was uplifting and fed my mind and soul. I particularly loved tuning in to Joyce Meyer, a television minister, who helped me slap my bad attitude into shape. One day she retold the New Testament story of Peter walking on water towards Jesus Christ. Peter was no less afraid than the other disciples, but he was willing to put his faith before his fears. And even when he began to doubt and sink, the Lord was right there to catch him, just like he is for us. I have had to work at putting my faith before my fears; but when I do, I can do things I never thought I could.

Shortly after he left our marriage, my ex-husband told me I would never marry again because I was such a "hermit." It hurt terribly. I am admittedly a bit introverted, preferring home, reading, writing, and hiking in the hills to just about any social activity. But still it hurt. The thought of dating again terrified me but after his comment I was determined to date. So, in a move that surprised even myself, I asked my friend and neighbor on a date. Being such a kind man, I knew he would make my initiation back into dating easy and safe. Also divorced, he understood my trepidation and my fragile heart. I called him my Codega man. During the Middle Ages, a Codega was a profession in Venice, Italy. People could hire a Codega to walk in front of them through the dark tunnels at night with a lantern, guiding their path home and protecting them from evil. My friend and Codega guided me through my dark time, for which I will always be grateful.

One of my biggest challenges was deciding what to do next with myself. Being a wife and mom of a large family doesn't leave much time for selfish pursuits; but now that my kids were grown and I was alone, I needed to rediscover myself. An article I read about divorce suggested that before making weighty decisions about your new future, you must take time to get emotionally healthy. The author advised that before settling down into a new life, a person should date twelve people and get six stamps in her passport. Practical or not, this new goal gave me something to focus on. I signed up for an online dating service and started looking at travel options. I had always dreamed of going to Italy with my husband; and as strange as it felt to go alone, I knew that I needed to find joy in my life, even if that meant doing things outside of my comfort zone.

I needed language credits for my degree and figured where better to learn Italian than Italy? I found a program in Rome that would fulfill my academic credits and give me a month-long vacation to boot! I took time off of work, cashed in a small retirement account, recruited a good friend to go with me, and set off on the best trip of my life! In reality, it was so much more than a trip. It was an investment in myself. During the week, we would stay in Rome, attending Italian classes in the morning and touring the city in the afternoon. On weekends we ventured off to Venice, Florence, and even a friend's beach house in Sicily. Making this dream come true was the best therapy I could ask for. It was the beginning of finding new confidence, direction, and enjoyment of life.

Around the same time, I met a man through an online dating site. He lived in another state, so most of our relationship developed online before we eventually met in person. He wrote me wonderful letters and even sent me roses after the first time we chatted online. My son had a great time teasing me over that; but they were the first flowers I'd received from a man in a very long time, so it was worth it! It was fun for a while, but carrying on a long distance relationship proved to be difficult, and he moved on. I did my crying yet again, then reminded myself I still had to date ten more men and get five more passport stamps in order to reach my goal. I wasn't really that serious about this silly goal—and if the right person had come along, I would have been happy to settle down before reaching number twelve. But he didn't, so this goal gave me something to keep me looking forward.

Eventually the time came that I could no longer afford to live in our family home. I agreed to move out and let my husband move in. I did not relish the thought of his new girlfriend taking over my home. After all the time and money we had jointly invested in building this home together, having him move in with another woman felt like one more betrayal. I was continually amazed at his thoughtlessness towards me during this process, but the days of him catering to my feelings were long over. My choices were limited, so I tried to think of this move as just another adventure. Still, I had my limits, and one day I hit mine—my personal breaking point where I could stand it no more. Before moving out of our family home to turn it over to my husband, I cleaned the home as I always do to prepare for the next owner. That is, until I came to the master bathroom. As I scrubbed the beautiful porcelain tub, the one I loved to take hot baths in, the one I picked out just for my husband and me, I realized that I was now cleaning my beloved bathtub for my husband and the new woman in his life. It was more than my heart could take. I stood up and called out to my son who was cleaning another area of the house, "Dad can clean the house, himself. We are leaving." And we left. We moved to a little house in town, and I spent the next three days curled in my bed, crying and feeling sorry for myself.

Divorce is like one big earthquake with lots of little aftershocks. Moving from our family home was a big aftershock. There was more damage to be done and more ways still to hurt. But it was also a turning point for me: a time to reassess my life, my attitude, and what I was going to do with all the sadness stored up in me. Up to this point, I had felt like a fly banging my head on a closed window. It was time to find the open door, even if it were a door that opened into a dark abyss.

I spent the next six months applying for jobs all over California and several other states. The interviews I was offered never felt quite right until I received one from a university in my hometown. In this job I would be surrounded by writers, something I loved and longed to do more of. I felt so strongly that this job was meant for me. I had my sister's husband give me a blessing the morning of my interview. I asked him to bless me that somehow, short of crying and begging, I would be able to secure this job. My confidence along with my faith waned, but I knew this was where I was supposed to be. I had felt God's hand guiding my life up to this point. I wanted to believe this would be a continuation of that. The image of Peter getting out of the boat kept coming to my mind. I just needed to get out of the safety of my boat, put my faith before my fears, and take the first step.

Two weeks later I was driving my life's belongings in my truck down to my new dream job. Everything was coming together: the job I prayed for, a new home close to my brother and sister and their families, and a new beginning. Exciting? Yes. Frightening? Yes. After a twelve-hour drive, I pulled into my new town, a bit lonely and tired at the thought of moving in and starting work the next morning. Feeling discouraged and alone, I stopped for dinner at a restaurant only to find two LDS missionaries standing at the counter. I was overcome with an undeniable feeling of being known. I knew I was being watched over by a loving Father in Heaven.

Two months later, I graduated from college and started to fill my life once more with new hopes and dreams.

I still struggle with the aftershocks of a failed marriage: financial devastation, loneliness, and sadness for myself and for my children. I'm only two years post-divorce, though (a relative newbie), and I'm still working on rebuilding my life. But I do know that it is because of my trials that I have become more dependent upon God and realize the awesome power He gives to my life.

I have also learned about the immense power of attitude. I decided early on that I did not want to define myself as a victim. I knew that was the sure path for bitterness and resentment to engulf me. Charles Swindoll's quote has inspired me to reach higher:

> The longer I live, the more I realize the impact of attitude on life. Attitude to me is more important than facts. It is more important than the past, than education, than money, than circumstances, than

failures, than success, than what other people think or say or do. It is more important than appearance, gift, or skill. It will make or break a company . . . a church . . . a home. The remarkable thing is we have a choice every day regarding the attitude we will embrace for that day. We cannot change our past . . . we cannot change the fact that people will act in a certain way. We cannot change the inevitable. The only thing we can do is play on the string we have, and that is our attitude. I am convinced that life is 10 percent what happens to me and 90 percent how I react to it. And so it is with you . . . we are in charge of our attitudes.

I think of this every time I am faced with a difficult circumstance or choice to make. It would be a lot easier if we could set our attitude on "positive" and never have to think about it again. But realistically, attitude, like faith, is a choice and a daily effort. It's a habit we develop through practice. I don't think it matters what kind of life trauma we are faced with, be it divorce, natural disaster, death, addiction, or illness. The attitude we choose determines our course and outcome. It can make the difference in whether we will be a victim or a victor.

17

Saving Bruce

My husband took our son Jack to see some golden retriever puppies that were ready for adoption. Jack sprawled out on the kitchen floor with the pups for a couple of hours, letting each pup crawl all around him, until finally he bonded to the little runt. The first night in our home, the puppy wouldn't eat. We weren't overly alarmed at the time; but by the second night, it was obvious something was not right. My husband took him back to the family we bought him from. Sure enough, he was ill, as were several of the other pups. Within three weeks, several of the puppies died.

This was just another disappointment to contend with. Our son no longer wanted a dog. He no longer wanted anyone or anything in his life that could cause him more pain. He was angry, depressed, and difficult to deal with. To make matters worse, it was about this time our rocky marriage began to crumble. For several months, our home seemed to sit under a dark cloud. I was hopeful that my husband and I could come out of this latest marital crisis as we had previously throughout our twenty-plus years. I held tightly to that hope. Our older three children were grown and had begun their independent lives elsewhere. Our youngest son was the only one home to witness the shattering of our marriage.

Surprisingly, Jack called me at work one day and announced he had found "his" dog. He said he knew this was the one that belonged with him. Jack asked me to come and help with the paperwork so he could bring the dog home. He sounded more chipper than he had in months. I wasn't sure it was a good idea with the circumstances at home. But this was suddenly so important to him, I was willing to keep an open mind.

I drove up to the pound, and Jack was in the parking lot playing with the dog. The dog was a Labrador and Akita mix. He was large, even at 4 months, and had a beautiful black coat with massive white paws. He was going to be put to sleep the next day, and my son was certain he needed to save the dog's life. Jack had already chosen a name before my arrival: Bruce, after Bruce Wayne, Batman's alter ego. It was destiny that Bruce would become our own canine superhero. I was so overwhelmed to see my son's face filled with joy that I couldn't say no to him. We brought Bruce home.

We didn't have a fence on our property, but Bruce gladly stayed near our house even when we weren't home. When we were home, he was a house dog. Even as a pup, Bruce was fairly passive and rarely barked. As he grew up, he became even more passive and loving. Bruce loved his walks, loved to run, and loved to be outside. But when he was indoors, he was happy to lay by our feet, nuzzle in our laps, and cuddle on our beds. Bruce slept with Jack every night. Jack was doing home school during this time, and he and Bruce became inseparable. Bruce went everywhere in the car with my son, quickly becoming his closest and best friend. Bruce was human-like in his emotions towards us. He seemed to be aware when we were having a hard time and would lay his head on our laps as if to console us.

Eventually my husband moved out of our home, and it was just Bruce, Jack, and me. Bruce was great company for both of us during that very difficult time. When my son would see me crying, he'd bring Bruce to me. Jack knew that was about all he could do, but somehow it was enough. My son would tell me he saved Bruce's life, and now Bruce was saving us.

Due to finances and the divorce settlement, I had to move out of our home. Jack, Bruce, and I moved to a small house that allowed dogs, but it did not have a yard. Bruce became even more of an indoor dog. Sometimes, when I was running late in the morning, I'd put him outside on the porch and tell him to go do his thing. But, Bruce never left the porch. He'd wait until someone would come with him.

I found a job in another city and was ready to move on with the next chapter of my life. Unfortunately, I wasn't able to bring Bruce with me. Jack made the decision to stay with Bruce and his dad, but it wasn't working out well. Our older son, Bryan, who was also living with his dad, promised to take care of Bruce if Jack decided to live with me. Jack and my daughter came to live with me that summer while they decided on colleges for the fall.

While I was on a trip with my mom and sister, my ex-husband decided to give Bruce away. The kids were devastated. Jack jumped in his car and started the twelve-hour drive home to see Bruce one more time. He only made it three hours when he was involved in a major car accident. My son wasn't hurt physically, but his car was totaled—and he didn't make it in time to see Bruce before he was sent away.

There were lots of tears about losing our sweet angel friend, Bruce. It was only a small consolation that he was in a good home. Bruce would not be forgotten, even a little bit, and there was always the hope that somehow he would be with us again. Several months later, my two boys were able to visit Bruce. Bryan and Jack got some closure and accepted the reality that Bruce had a new home. I thought that was the end of the story.

Just a few weeks later, Bryan, who had moved back to his own home in Tahoe, was back at his dad's for a dental appointment. He spent the night at his father's home, and the two of them had a disagreement that evening. The next morning, his father left a note on Bryan's bed that said he wasn't welcome there, anymore. Bryan was heartbroken. He had moved into a home in Tahoe that allowed pets and felt he needed a companion to comfort him.

Bryan decided to go to the same pound where Jack had originally found Bruce. As he walked through the animal shelter checking out dogs, there was Bruce! Poor Bruce had been there for over a week. It wasn't likely the pound would have kept him much longer. It was frightening to think that had Bryan not found Bruce that day, he would have been put down without any of us knowing. We later learned that Bruce had run away from his new owners, and the animal control people had found him. We were overjoyed when Bryan brought Bruce home, again!

We all believe that Heavenly Father put Bruce in our lives to give us the love and comfort we needed to get through a very difficult time. I am so glad my son listened to those tender promptings to go to the pound that day. Both boys feel that Bruce saved their lives with his love and comforting devotion. And in return, my sons saved Bruce's life twice!

18

Heartache, Betrayal, Forgiveness, Recovery

It is an understatement to say that finding myself divorced after 28 years of marriage was a shock. I was raised in a deeply religious LDS family and married into the same. Even in my large extended family we had somehow managed to escape divorce. I suppose, like most people, I never thought it would happen to me. It did.

From the time I met my to-be-husband, we seemed in most ways compatible. We shared the same values, hopes, and dreams. After marriage, children came quickly, and our relationship seemed to strengthen with the birth of each child. Disagreements were few and far between. The only blemish on our otherwise fairy tale life was my husband's excessive jealousy over any man in my previous life. My family could not even utter the name of an old boyfriend without me incurring punishment. I should have taken this as a warning sign, but I didn't. I chalked it up to at best a compliment, and at worst a little controlling.

Following the birth of our fifth and final son, financial success entered our lives. It was the result of honest hard work, but with it crept in a sense of materialism and entitlement. No longer was a nice home and average comforts sufficient for my husband; he needed more. One motorcycle was not enough; he needed four. He learned to play the guitar, but once again one was not enough; he collected fifteen. And so it went. I suspected it was a phase he was going through, but "things" became a more significant part of what he valued than before. As his business interests became more organized, free time became more plentiful. Time he used to spend working was now free to explore things that had not previously been part of his life.

Unfortunately, they were not things that build up a marriage. What started out as "perusing girly magazines" turned into a serious pornography addiction. From there came demands for more uncomfortable and degrading sexual relations with me. He no longer appreciated the intimacy of our formerly close marital relationship. I went along with it for a while but soon realized that I could not endure the demands of his fantasies. Along with these changes came a notable decrease in his commitment to our religion and values. Our family was still in tact, but our lives were growing apart.

My husband's sudden increase in "business trips" caught my attention. It usually necessitated him leaving on weekends and staying at hotels where contacting him by phone was "impossible." It didn't take long to put those pieces together with the unusual credit card charges and cell phone bills. And as if to confirm any remaining doubt, the clerk at our local photo shop unknowingly returned to me several rolls of developed film turned in earlier by my husband. The clerk's expression blanched when he realized the woman in the photos was not, in fact, me. That night I built a fire in the fireplace and burned each photo, one by one. It gave me some degree of satisfaction watching their affair, or at least the cruel evidence of it, go up in flames.

After that, the typical pattern ensued: I confronted, he denied, evidence prevailed, he admitted. I was both crushed and angry that he would do this to me and to our family. For the first time in our relationship, the possibility entered my mind that our marriage may not make it. Sensing my doubt, he showered me with promises that I desperately wanted to believe, and I resigned to stay the course and try to repair our marriage.

Within weeks of his forced confession, I became ill with what I would soon discover was a venereal disease. Thankfully it was curable, but knowing he had risked my health for his pleasure and convenience added insult to already serious injury. Again he showed convincing remorse, promised this behavior would never be repeated, and vowed to seek help from our bishop. Once again, I forged on, determined to see this through for the sake of our family.

Up to this point I had endured his betrayal alone without speaking of it to anyone. I believed that he was genuinely remorseful and that he wanted our marriage to work. Beyond that, I was embarrassed by my husband's deviance; and if we did stay together, I didn't want anyone to know just how far he had lowered himself. Gratefully though, it was around this time that a good friend noticed that I did not seem like myself and offered a listening ear. I finally felt safe disclosing the burdens of my broken heart with her, and the relief that came from sharing my heavy load was the first of many mercies that preserved my sanity and allowed me to go on.

My husband and I both agreed to marriage counseling, and to some degree it helped. On the surface, things looked better, but the whisperings of the Spirit continued to warn me that things were not right. After months of believing that our marriage was improving and that his infidelities had ceased, I received a telephone call from his mistress. She had the impudence to inquire as to why I would not grant my husband the divorce she claimed he had been demanding of me. My heart and stomach sank as if the bottom had just fallen out of my world. My husband had never mentioned divorce, let alone demanded it. Apparently I was not the only woman on the receiving end of his lies, although that gave me little comfort. As I ended this unwelcome conversation, my sons couldn't help but notice my distress. I collapsed in their arms and confided to them their father's infidelities. Telling my children led to telling my parents and siblings. As hard as this was, their love and support were like a balm to my open wounds. It felt so good to be understood and receive the comfort my soul longed for.

The difficult part was hearing my own family plead with me to not leave my husband. I expected my sons might defend their father if only to keep their family in tact, but even my mother discouraged me from considering divorce because of the pain it would bring my children. Unable to hurt them more than they had already been hurt, I put my feelings aside; and with all the energy I could muster, I rededicated myself to making our marriage work. I demanded certain requirements, again, before I committed to reinvest my trust. These included a promise that all contact with the other woman would cease and that he would continue in counseling, participate more fully in our religion, and be more present at home as a husband and father. He agreed.

For months my husband appeared as if he were trying to save our marriage, but suspicious behaviors continued along with spiritual warnings from the Spirit. One night, at a loss for what to do, I poured out my soul to the Lord. I pleaded for help to discern what course of action I should take with my life. A welcome peace came over me, and I slept soundly for a few hours until I was awakened with a precise sense of certain actions I needed to take the next day. Specifically, the impression came to my mind that I must open a separate bank account, make a deposit of $3,500, retain a lawyer, and get our home appraised. I hesitated in disbelief, prayed to know if this was indeed the Lord's will, and immediately received the same prompting again. The next day, I deposited $3,500 in a new bank account and set off to see an attorney. After reviewing the necessary steps to begin divorce proceedings, he informed me that his retainer fee would be $3,500. I stood in disbelief and gratitude that the Lord directed me so personally and precisely. I felt an exhilarating reassurance that He was guiding my every step and that I was on my way to taking control of my life again.

Throughout the following year, there were multiple recurrences of my husband's infidelity. Remorse always followed and always left me wondering if this time was the right time to terminate this unbearable situation. My sons continued to plead with me to forgive their father again, promising on his behalf that this really would be his last offense. How sorry I felt for our sons to be placed in this unconscionable position of not just knowing of their father's transgressions but having to defend them for the sake of their own security. The mother in me could not bring myself to hurt them more than they were already hurting, so I persevered another year. I looked for anything I could do differently in our marriage, anything we hadn't tried that might help. No stone was left unturned. I was willing to try anything; but I had quietly resolved that if his behavior did not improve, then I would not allow myself to suffer indefinitely.

I can say without hesitation that I would not have survived this difficult time were it not for my faith in God. Even if my husband didn't love me, I knew my Savior did. As I turned to my Savior, I felt His power easing my burden and strengthening my soul. I knew He was aware of my situation and would guide me through it. I felt great comfort as I attended the temple each week and found solace in that holy place. Inspired music lifted my soul and gave me hope to endure another day. The Atonement of Jesus Christ took on new meaning as I read the scriptures and was guided to words that calmed my troubled heart and gave me hope. He understood my suffering. Even if my marriage ended, I now knew I would be fine. I knew I was not alone.

Several months passed without incident; and just as I was beginning to believe that my husband was truly committed to me and our marriage, my worst nightmare reappeared, this time on my front porch. I had just returned from a trip with my husband to visit our sons, who were away at school in Utah. I returned home two days before my husband only to receive a most unwelcome visit at my own home by my husband's mistress. She came bearing videotapes as proof of their affair and of his commitment to her. I watched the tape; and while my stomach turned and my grief was immeasurable, I shed no tears. My resolve was now sure and unshakable. I phoned my husband to inform him that I was done. The next day I filed for divorce.

Ironically, my husband was furious at his mistress for doing such a thing to me. Somehow he was able to overlook his part in the affair and pin the worst of the offense on her. Promises of "never again" flowed freely from his lips once more; and this time, the contention between the two of them almost convinced me that their relationship might finally be over. Once again I hung on and did not carry through with the divorce. Somehow I allowed my husband to convince me that if I divorced him it would be my fault for ruining the family. I now see that as the manipulation it was intended to be, but at the time I bought into the guilt trip.

Yet again, this other woman who was still in my husband's life had the nerve to confront me and pressure me towards divorce. I had the divorce papers drawn up; but upon attempting to deliver them, I was met by my husband, his parents, and my sons, all of whom begged me to give him another chance. I felt desperate to move on with my life; but once again I succumbed to my sons' pleadings—this time with the understanding that if the infidelity continued, I would have my sons' support in leaving. When my fourth son left for his mission he said to me in parting, "If you have to divorce Dad while I'm gone, I understand." My husband reassured him, "Don't worry, Son, Mom and I will work it all out." Naïve as it sounds now, his words gave me hope that he meant it. As anyone can now predict, he did not.

Before long, the suspicious business trips were back, along with incriminating phone records. Their affair was alive and well, and I was done for good. I said goodbye. This time, I meant it. I put together the divorce papers, put the house up for sale, informed my sons it was over, and prepared myself to move ahead with my life. My husband was stunned. Within one week the house had sold and I had purchased another home and began to pack—all while he begged for yet another chance.

Something about this time was different. Not only did I have my sons' unwavering support, I had a personal reassurance that the time had come for me to move on. No more excuses. No more exceptions. No more wondering if he might change or if I hadn't done enough. No more living in perpetual disappointment. The end was here, and I was okay.

Before the divorce was final, a dear friend invited me to tour England with her for five days. I could not have predicted what a liberating and healing experience it would be to separate myself from the circumstances that had held me hostage to heartache for so long. I felt like I had sprouted wings and could fly! The divorce was finalized in March of 2001, just shy of our 28th wedding anniversary. Unlike many divorce situations, he treated me fairly with the split of our finances. Although it necessitated me having to seek employment for the first time in my married life, I did have a home and food to eat.

I did the best I could in my marriage and loved unconditionally. He had made the decisions that ended our marriage, and I had suffered enough. I was not going to carry the pain, anymore. I would not allow him to be the reason for any further unhappiness. It was simply over!

Looking back now, I can see clearly the strengths and buffers that saw me through that treacherous time:

First and foremost is the positive mental attitude I was able to maintain. Even during the stormiest times, it allowed me to see the good in life and keep going.

My religious upbringing taught me that I must rely on the Lord and make sure I am living correctly. With that in place, I know I will always prevail.

And the most profoundly powerful thing I did to allow me to heal and move on was to follow the admonition of Jesus Christ when he said, "I will forgive whom I will forgive, but of you it is required to forgive all men" (D&C 64:10). As difficult as that seems in the throes of divorce, there is simply no other way to move forward except with a forgiving heart. I had to let go of the bitterness, for my sake especially. When my now ex-husband asked for my forgiveness, I had to decide whether or not I could and would; but in the end, I knew that if I were ever to get my life in proper balance again, I had to start here.

As it turned out, I had an easier time moving on than my husband. Even after our divorce, and while living with his girlfriend, he continued to plead with me to put our family back together. I knew my course now, and I was prepared to move ahead with my life. I took stock of where I had been and how far I had come, and I felt remarkably whole.

I never hesitated to believe that I was capable of loving and being loved again. I had been through so much pain for so many years that I was looking forward to a happier chapter of my life. Still, I never would have predicted that I would find love through a church-based dating website. No sooner had I indicated that I was looking for "the perfect man," I received a letter from a man in New York assuring me that "he was indeed that perfect man."

This incredible man has brought laughter back into my life. He helped to heal my wounds and opened up a new world of joy to me. This was not by coincidence. I know that a loving Father was very aware of me and what I had endured. He was also aware of this good man who had suffered a similar heartache of an unfaithful spouse followed by eleven years alone working through his own journey towards forgiveness. We have now been together ten wonderful years; and today we enjoy holidays with his ex-spouse, her husband, and all of our children. I have come to consider his former wife a true friend. I hope that one day the association with my former husband will be as cordial; but for now, we have no problem being together in family situations. The healing and recovery have been amazing. Especially where children are involved, there is no other course that can result in real recovery. I am grateful that my former husband has returned to the Church and is now living his life in a way his sons can be proud of.

I know now that life is too short to be miserable and too long to have every day be a reminder of yesterday's pain. My life is rich and full and blessed, and I am happy.

19

The Cost of Divorce

The most stressful, expensive, and emotionally draining experience of my life was, without a doubt, the long, drawn-out divorce battle my former husband and I endured for years on end. Never did I plan or wish for my marriage to end in divorce, especially after having two beautiful children together, our thirteen-year-old daughter and ten-year-old son.

The heartache and disappointment of a broken marriage and becoming a "divorced mom" was enough to suffer; but the fact that our financial settlement was not ordered for over three years after our divorce settlement was finalized added immeasurable stress to our fractured family. In my experience, the court system, attorneys, judges, and guardian ad litem never seemed to care much about getting financial orders in place in a timely manner. What a difference it would have made, though, in improving the quality of our lives!

Beyond the mental, emotional, and spiritual costs, divorce often brings with it enormous and overwhelming financial costs. What compels me to share my experience is that I know we are not the only divorced family that has had this devastating experience financially and with the legal system. For all the protections it provides, it often comes at a high price financially and temporally. Delays are followed by more delays, and fees stack up on top of fees. Our family, like many others I know, came all too close to losing everything in this process.

The fact that my ex-husband did not pay any alimony or child support left me as the sole provider for our children. He devised a strategy in which he would "plead poverty" to the courts, claiming that he was living in his car—when in reality he was living in a nice home, free from the responsibility of taking care of us. He successfully lied his way through the legal system, at our expense.

Fortunately, I am a hard-working person and had years of work experience in my back pocket. I sought full-time work, often working overtime to keep myself and my children safe and comfortable. The mother bear in me knew I had no choice but to protect and provide.

It took my ex-husband's joining the Army years after our divorce for our situation to improve. Thankfully, the Army took it upon themselves to garnish my ex-husband's wages, and I began to receive the child and spousal support that was originally ordered but ignored all these years. What a blessing! Included in my payments via the military were also my ex-husband's arrears—what a blessed surprise! I will always be grateful that our U.S. Military requires men and women to fulfill their financial obligations to family. How nice it would be if all employers required their employees to be current on spousal and child support. Our society would be better off in so many ways.

Among the valuable lessons learned from this frustrating experience with our legal system is that we must be self-reliant and persistent. We cannot always count on the legal system to ensure that alimony and child support will be determined and paid in a timely way. As in my case, it can take years before any of it is enforced. I would tell anyone in my position to do all you can to make sure all orders are put into place. Beyond that, do all that you can to become self-reliant in taking care of yourself and your children. With the Lord's help, you can do this!

It feels wonderful to know that I can take good care of myself and my family. I have the confidence of a survivor and am committed to being a good example to others, especially to my family and friends. I am committed to enduring all things with grace, dignity, and lots of hope and faith in the Lord. With that knowledge, everything will be okay. It truly will.

20

My Children Are #1

Facing divorce is a difficult place to be, especially as a mother of two young children. It is challenging and scary, to say the least. My daughter was 13 and my son was 10 when our lives changed forever. In that moment of staring divorce in the face, I committed to myself that I would always be there for my children. I would always put them first, no matter what!

I was forty-four years old at the time, and I was left to provide for and protect our two young children on my own, all alone. I was left to meet all of their needs, alone. Tragically, my children's father chose not to be a part of their lives and rejected his legal and moral responsibilities to care for, protect, and provide for our children. From the time of our divorce, he was emotionally, financially, and physically absent. This most important duty had been handed to me and me alone. The heartache, disappointment, and feelings of abandonment and rejection our children suffered were excruciating to watch. They grew up believing that their father's love for them was conditional.

As my children were left to cope with the consequences of their dad's choices, I remained the one they could count on, no matter what. I was their shoulder to cry on, their support, their constant. I was there for them unconditionally, and I believe that blessed them with security, love, and a reassurance that they would be okay. And they were. I took care of them and the Lord took care of all of us.

Despite the pain of our loss, I am forever grateful that I could be there for my daughter and son. I knew I had one chance to raise my children, and I wanted to give them all I had with no regrets. Loving our children is the most important gift we can give. It was challenging when life turned my world upside-down, but keeping my eye single to the wellbeing of my children was my number one focus through it all. It still is. I am there for them now and forever. They know this.

Our son and daughter are older now. They survived those painful years and are thriving as fine young adults. Their father has had an "awakening" of sorts and is making his way back into our children's lives. While his past actions do not give me complete confidence, I am grateful for his apparent change of heart and hope that he will continue to choose to be there for them. Both of our children have openly and lovingly welcomed their father back into their lives. Talk about unconditional love! This is an amazing and wonderful gift they have given to their father, to themselves, and to me. They are wondrous examples of pure love.

An important element in helping me heal from my divorce was learning to own my part in the divorce. I began by verbally acknowledging my mistakes to my ex-husband and my children. I then had to forgive myself. This was difficult work. After owning my contribution to the unraveling of our family, I had to accept that I am not perfect, nor does the Lord expect that I will be. I allowed the Lord to teach me and help me heal and grow from all I had been through. I kept living the best life I could, staying true to what I believed and who I wanted to be. As I stayed close to the Lord, He stayed close to me.

The other person I had to learn to forgive was my ex-husband. This continues to be an ongoing exercise. I have to be consistently willing to forgive him in the new and different situations and experiences we continue to face with him. Forgiveness is an exercise that we must repeatedly pursue, sometimes daily.

I know there are many like me who have had to be both mother and father figure to our children, but we are never alone. Not only was the Lord my constant support, my family and friends were there for me through my worst times. They comforted me and helped me navigate my way through the difficult waters I had to go through—not around, but through.

The lesson I keep with me today is the power of love. I came through my hardest trial with increased faith, hope, and a new understanding of the awesome power of love. My children and I will love one another unconditionally forever, no matter what. That is the kind of love that heals and triumphs. In the end, it is truly all about love.

21

My Road to Peace

Years ago, I was in a marriage that was struggling to survive the destructive ills of infidelity, betrayal, hurt, resentment, and loss of trust and respect. After thirteen years of marriage and four children, my husband began having an affair with a woman from work. I initially thought it was just a flirtatious relationship; and since I have never been the jealous type, I let it go. As time went on, I began to suspect there was more going on than I knew. Because we lived in a small town, our family knew and even socialized with this woman and her family. I would often catch what felt like intimate glances between my husband and this other woman. Warning bells went off in my head, but I dismissed them, convincing myself that I was overreacting. There was nothing in me that could imagine my husband having an affair with another woman. I couldn't even conceive of him lying to me!

Over the next few weeks and months, I came to suspect that their relationship was indeed real—and I could feel him moving further and further away from me. I was sad for myself but afraid for him and the dangerous path he was on. I felt an urgency to end it quickly before too much damage occurred. I figured he was having a mid-life crisis and told my husband that I thought his relationship with this woman was inappropriate. He assured me they were just friends and said that I was overreacting. This is what I had hoped he would say, so I dropped the issue and tried to be an understanding wife. Warning bells continued to go off, however, and I knew in my heart that my husband was lying to me. I began checking up on him, searching for any evidence that would verify my suspicions. Sadly, I didn't have to look far or for long. I confronted him with evidence I thought would bring him to his knees, knock some sense into him, and get him to confess and get back on the right track so we could save our family. To the contrary, he only denied it and got angry with me for being "judgmental and vindictive." This became the cycle we would repeat again and again for the next four years.

The hurt I felt was beyond anything I could have ever imagined. I felt pain that I never knew existed. I couldn't sleep. I lost a tremendous amount of weight. I carried a constant ache deep within my soul. Yet, through all of this I was determined not to let this evil get the best of my family. I often reflected on the scripture that says, "Greater love hath no man than this, that a man lay down his life for his friends" (John 15:13). At one time my husband had been my very best friend. I loved him then and now, and I could think of no better way to show my love for him than to "lay down my life" for him. So, I waited. My life as I knew it had been shattered, anyway, and I was willing to live a life in pieces to get my children's father back into our family. I didn't want him to lose out on the blessings of his family. I wanted my kids to have their dad. I wanted my husband back. I thought my love could fix this.

My kids often asked about their dad's unusual behavior, but even when they were angry with him I would protect him. I didn't want my kids to have to carry the hurt and betrayal that I was feeling; they were such heavy, black, ugly feelings. I hoped my husband would change his ways before the heaviness settled on my kids. I wanted my kids to be proud of their dad and to be able to love him without any misgivings. Little did I know that all of this would backfire on me.

My husband eventually confessed his affair to me. He came home from work one day panicked, begging me not to answer the phone. I promised, and he proceeded to tell me that I was right all along, that he had been sleeping with the woman from work. But he was also sleeping with another woman. His current distress (and apparently his sole motivation for telling me) was that the two women had recently found out about each other and had set out on a plan to destroy him by telling me. He wanted to tell me his version of the story before the two women did. I listened with hope that this was the turning point I had prayed for. I never did answer the phone; and not only that, I substitute taught his class in order to spare him from having to face the two women. At last, I thought, this nightmare was over and we could start picking up the pieces and putting our marriage back together. I had faith that if we both applied the principles of the Atonement, we could rebuild. I had faith that the Atonement could fix even this mess. What I didn't realize was that my husband didn't have the same faith. His solution was to run away from God and the Church. He asked me to move away from our home, family, and friends to a place where we could be anonymous. He proposed a plan in which we would leave the Church "for a couple of years" and then come back to activity—all would be fixed. I knew better. I knew that running away from the one thing that could fix this mess would leave us with no chance of surviving in tact. Without two people applying the Atonement, there was not a lot that could be done to repair our marriage.

After 18 years, our marriage finally ended in divorce. As painful as that was, the actual divorce did not mark the end of my pain. As time went on, my two older children developed resentment and anger towards me and decided to live with their dad. They accused me of being unforgiving, vindictive, and evil, treating me as though I had been the cause of the break-up of our home. In their minds, none of this would have happened if I hadn't been so "churchy." That was a blow I was not prepared for. I naively thought that after all the protecting and sacrificing I had done for my husband, my children would see me as the good guy in all of this; but they didn't. They were hurt and were led to believe it was my fault. Not only did I lose my home and husband, but I also lost my once close and trusting relationships with my children. My broken heart felt as though it would never mend.

I wanted so desperately to set things right and start on the road to healing. My soul hungered for peace, but how I was going to get it I did not know. My mind mercilessly replayed every scenario that had caused me pain and suffering, which only reminded me how terribly unfair things had turned out. To my eyes, my ex-husband had not suffered anything near what I had suffered. His selfish decisions had put us in this situation, yet I was the one paying for it. I found myself trying to come up with ways to make it fair. I spent a lot of time wishing bad things would come to him so that he would suffer the consequences I thought he deserved. I thought this would bring me the peace of mind I so desperately wanted.

Eventually I realized that replaying past events in my mind and wishing ill for my ex-husband were getting me nowhere. I wanted to heal, and I wanted to be a healthy mom for my kids. I began to accept that in this lifetime things would not be fair. Everything beyond my own choices was out of my control, so I needed to let it go. I had to quit spending energy imagining ways he could "get his." I had to turn it over to the Lord. I had to trust in Him.

Knowing the Plan of Salvation, I knew that one day my husband would stand before the judgment bar of God to be judged—and that was the time for justice to be served, not now and not by me. Initially, I took a certain amount of comfort in the thought that suffering would come to him one way or another, if not in this life, then the next. This was pivotal in helping me let go of my need for control. It helped me to begin turning my burdens over to the Lord. For the first time I began to heal. I felt greater strength and like I was finally moving forward. I was more open to the teachings and whisperings of the Spirit, because I wasn't cluttering my mind with useless vengeance. I felt better, although I knew I wasn't completely whole. There was still another step that needed to be taken.

I had studied much about forgiveness and charity. I knew that along with the gift of charity came peace. I prayed often for charity and worked diligently on forgiving. As I turned my burdens over to the Lord, I was finally able to forgive. I would let the Lord pass judgment; and as much as I looked forward to that day, I no longer felt that I was responsible for ensuring things were fair. That was the Lord's responsibility, and He would do it. I washed my hands of judging my ex-husband's choices, and it felt good.

The final piece came together years after my divorce as I was talking with my current husband about the difficult work of forgiveness. He said something that changed my life and made all the difference in finding real peace. "I know you," he said, "And I know your heart. When you are standing before the judgment bar of God, I know you will forgive him. So you might as well let go of it now and enjoy your life." I pondered that, picturing myself standing before the judgment bar of God as a witness against this man who had hurt me so deeply. I saw myself rehearsing all the betrayals I had experienced at his hand. Then I saw his face as God declared His judgment and the consequences that would follow. I saw his suffering and his sorrow, and tears began to fall down my cheeks. My heart was softened in a way I had never anticipated it could be. I actually ached as I imagined his suffering, and I could no longer bear the pain. Suddenly everything I had suffered paled in comparison to my ex-husband's suffering, and I felt compassion. I realized then that when it came down to it, I would take no joy in seeing another person suffer such pain and regret, even my ex-husband. I knew I would ask the Lord to intervene and extend forgiveness, because I could not bear to watch his suffering. My sweet new husband was right: if I were going to let go of all the pain and ill will toward my ex-husband in the end, I might as well start now.

The power of the Atonement has worked mighty miracles in my life. I no longer find comfort in hoping for a heavy dose of justice in the next life. I now have great peace, as I have experienced the unconditional love of my Heavenly Father. There are still rough spots on the road I travel; but I have learned to trust in the Lord and to bask in His love. I have also learned that great joy comes when I allow others the same privilege. Now I am truly at peace.

22

Permission to Love

I am not a child of divorce, but my five children are. From the beginning of the deterioration of our marriage, I have been concerned about its effects on our children. I have tried to listen and understand what they are going through, but sometimes it takes a mother a long time to discern and comprehend her children's deepest concerns.

Every time I discover a trusted Latter-day Saint adult who is also a child of divorce, I ask him what his parents did to help him survive such a devastating loss. Without exception, I receive the same answer: "Don't say anything bad about the other parent in front of the children."

It seems so simple. I tell myself this is something I can and must do for my children's sake but sometimes my ability to do just that has been stretched to the limit.

A few weeks before my husband and I separated, it became necessary to take my children, ages 2 through 12, away from our home for a while. My husband had typically been a good father; but lately, for reasons yet unknown to me, he had become hostile and out of control. He frightened all of us, and I was genuinely concerned for our safety. As we made our escape, I drove around the city in no particular direction. We were all sobbing. "What do I say to my children?" I silently prayed.

In a flash of inspiration I did not fully comprehend at the time, I tried to explain their role in the situation. Struggling to control my voice, I said, "Daddy is not thinking clearly right now, so we need to leave for a while. You are safe. And now you children have a job to do. Can you think what it might be?"

My twelve-year-old began, "We have to make Daddy see what he is doing."

"No," I gently interrupted, "That's not your job to make Daddy see anything."

My ten-year-old gave it a try, "We have to get Mom and Dad back together."

"That's Mom and Dad's job, honey, not yours," I reminded him.

The car was quiet except for a few soft sobs. I gathered all my courage and said, "You children have one job, and that is *to love*. Love your dad. Love your mom. Love each other. And love yourselves. It is not your job to take care of Mom or Dad or to fix our marriage. *You are to love.* It would be nice if you got good grades in school and practiced your instruments and kept your rooms clean; but if you can't do anything else, just love." Everyone in the car, including me, relaxed. None of us knew *how* to love my husband in these circumstances, but we knew it was the right thing to do.

A year later, it was my son who taught *me* how and why I needed to help them love their father. We were struggling to know how to handle a delicate situation. The children were going to the dedication of the Oquirrh Mountain Temple with their father. He called to say he couldn't attend. I volunteered to go with them, but the children were concerned that Dad would be upset if I went in his place. So they decided not to go at all. I was angry that my children would miss out on a sacred opportunity because they were worried about offending their dad. I started to lecture all of them about the need to "stand up" to their dad. My son, with great emotion, said, "Mom, you don't understand. You are no longer with Dad. You don't have to deal with him, but we do. What he says and thinks affects us. When you two disagree, we have to absorb that."

I choked on my retort. What my son needed most at that moment was my permission for him to love his father. I use the word "love," but I also mean forgiveness, patience, and giving someone the benefit of the doubt. In other words, charity. My son needed to see the good in his father. He needed to find joy and happiness with his dad, too. All the children were craving kindness, reconciliation, and hope—for themselves and their father. I needed to change my thinking.

I now understood the driving force behind the concept of not badmouthing my children's dad. It came down to this: My children need my permission to love their father and, thereby, to love themselves. Everyone makes mistakes, both children and parents; sometimes those mistakes deeply hurt the people around us, but we are all still worthy of love. We don't have to love the mistakes, but we can love the people making them.

When we love someone, it doesn't authorize him or her to dominate, belittle, or take advantage of us. He or she may continue these practices, but love does not condone them. We can take steps to protect ourselves and others; however, we must choose to not let anger, hate, and resentment permeate our lives. We can choose gentleness in the midst of harshness, silence in the face of shouts, and cooperation in answer to accusations. Isn't this what the Savior is trying to teach all of us? Charity, the pure love of Christ, can overcome anything. 1 Peter 4:8 says, "And above all things have fervent charity among yourselves: for charity shall cover the multitude of sins."

My children and I also learned that love may or may not inspire someone else to make corrections in his or her life. Love may not change the other person, but it will change me. Love can heal *all* hurts! It has been said that resentment is like taking poison and waiting for the other person to die. Love is the antidote.

In a quiet moment, I asked my children in what specific ways I have helped them to love both their father and mother. My oldest daughter said she appreciated that I don't compete with her dad for their love. I don't try to outdo their dad by having something "bigger and better" at my house. My son said he was so glad Dad and I don't fight, anymore. As parents we discuss matters concerning the children in a cooperative manner. If that is not possible, we deliberately end the conversation before it gets too heated. For my littlest children, it helps them when I am enthusiastic about their time with their dad. Early on, we established a routine leading up to their time with Dad. I give them a hug goodbye, put on some bright lipstick, and give them a kiss in the middle of their hand. Just like in the endearing children's story, we call it "the kissing hand." I have even been known to do a silly tap dance or smash my face against the house window in a funny pose as they drive down the street in Dad's car. My hope is that all of these little things send a message to my children that they are loved and have permission to love and be happy no matter where they are or who they are with.

Learning to love has been a blessing in our lives. Although it did not save my marriage, it saved my family. My children have healthy relationships with both their father and their mother. My former husband and I are good partners in the raising of our children. None of us is perfect. We just do our best each day, and love makes up the difference.

23

Letting Go

We have a tradition in my family of origin—a little dangerous, but thrilling and fun. Every New Year's Day, we gather at my parents' horse pasture. We saddle up a couple of horses, attach ropes to the saddles, and take turns pulling each other behind on saucers. The real thrill comes when the person on the saucer is taken to the meadow and pulled around in circles until he almost falls off; then the horseman gallops up a small hill, causing the sledder to shoot up in the air. We haven't lost anyone, yet, and we share a lot of laughs.

We have another tradition in my family of origin—again, thrilling and fun, but for me it became more than a little dangerous. We stay married, no matter what. No matter how difficult the relationship, we stick it out. We don't abandon our commitments. It is a wonderful tradition and has blessed my family members for generations. We give marriage our joyful effort, patient endurance, quiet faith, unselfish sacrifice, and sometimes grumpy compliance. Divorce is never an option.

One year, the events of my life collided with these two traditions with such force that it propelled me to do the hardest thing I have ever done: let my husband go. We had been married only three years when my husband first brought up the idea of divorce. We had been fighting a lot. I was exhausted trying to care for our two little children. He felt that my asking him to spend less time playing computer games and more time helping out at home was demanding and "trying to wear the pants in the family." When he first uttered the word "divorce," I was horrified. We had a temple marriage (I thought that was supposed to be some kind of inoculation against divorce); and with the threat of divorce hanging in the air, I backed down immediately and stayed in "my place." I tried my best to be a supportive wife and not "cause" any more fights.

Life plodded on, but I walked on eggshells much of the time. We had three more children. When I did have an opinion different from my husband's, I would occasionally stand my ground—but more often, the argument would end with him threatening divorce and me doing anything I could to get him to change his mind. Apparently the threat was part strategy, as he later admitted to my parents that the best way to get me to do what he wanted was to mention divorce.

Threats of divorce were infrequent at first. He dropped them like bombs about once a year. Then it became every six months. Eventually he added that he would quit his job or even commit suicide if I didn't do exactly as he said. By the time we were married 12 years, the threats came almost every month. It became so common that I could predict when he would lash out. But common or not, I was still terrified. I was a stay-at-home mom with five young children and no other job experience. How could I survive without a husband? No one in my family had ever divorced, and I was not about to let it start with me.

The situation deteriorated quickly, however. Life with him became surreal. And scary. One night as I was reading in bed, my husband came upstairs after playing computer games, knelt beside the bed, and through clenched teeth whispered, "I want to hurt you." I sat shocked in an eerie kind of quiet. I asked if he meant emotionally or physically. He laughed, "Like you have hurt me.

You don't deserve to be loved. You don't deserve friends or family to support you. You deserve to be alone and in pain." My husband was convinced I was to blame for the consequences his actions were starting to reap. I was not. He had brought this on himself. It was his choices that were bringing him so much pain and his actions that had alienated his family and friends, but he had lost touch with reality.

The next few days were a nightmare. My husband threatened to kick me out of the house, because in his mind it was his. To him, the fact that I didn't earn any money meant that I contributed nothing to the family. In his eyes, I was therefore worth nothing. His behavior was getting increasingly out of control, and I worried for our children and myself. I often made arrangements for them to go to a friend's house after school until dinner time. One day, when I told the children of the arrangements for that afternoon, they questioned why. I replied that I just wanted them to have fun. My eight-year-old, not so easily fooled, countered, "Is it because Daddy has been saying mean things to you again?"

My face dropped, "Yes," I admitted. She started to cry. She said she was afraid. Her dad didn't say mean things to her, so I asked why she felt that way. My perceptive and wise daughter answered, "I know, but as soon as he is done with you, he will start on us." I knew she was right.

What kept me in the marriage so long was hope and faith in a family tradition that told me if I hung on long enough he would change. It would get better. I would not be a quitter. I would keep my covenants no matter what. It would be better to have a poor marriage than no marriage at all. I wanted to believe that.

That evening he shoved me in front of the kids. Frightened and dazed, I called our neighbor, a police officer, for advice. He advised me to get out of the house immediately. I resisted, reminding him this was his friend we were talking about.

"I know," he said, but still insisted I leave. "He will shove you at first, then he'll start hitting. And it will only get worse until it's too late. Get out now." I gathered the children and ran.

I separated from my husband but inside kept hanging on, believing that at some point my husband would "come to his senses." The threats didn't stop, however, even months after our initial separation. In fact, they got worse. But I wanted to be strong. A year and a half went by, but I refused to give up on our marriage.

New Year's Day came around again, and the kids and I were sledding with my family. My oldest nephew was pulling me behind the horse, doing circles in the meadow. The first time around, I wiped out in the snow. We laughed it off and I tried again, this time falling off on the second circle in the snow. I took a breather and warmed up with some hot chocolate before gathering my courage for one more turn. As we approached the meadow, I said to myself, "I will hang on no matter what. I am strong. I can do this." As I swirled around, my grip tightened, and I flipped up in the air and landed on my back. Still I would not let go. My saucer long gone, the horse was now dragging me upside down through the deep snow. There, on that cold and bouncy ride, I had a sudden revelation: "This could kill me. I need to let go."

I looked like the abominable snow monster as I walked up the hill. Everyone, including me, was laughing. But my inner laughter stopped. I realized this family tradition was not very healthy for me—on a sled or in my marriage. It was time to let go of my husband. Maybe he would never go so far as to kill me, but he was burying me, emotionally and spiritually. His actions were destroying my soul, and that was unacceptable for me and for my children. I had given marriage my whole effort. I had held on for so long, but now there was nothing more I could do. I had to let go. And what's more, I now knew *it was okay to let go.*

Being dragged behind someone is fun on a saucer in the snow, but in a healthy marriage there should be two people pulling their own weight and lifting each other up. They don't have to do it perfectly, but there should be no dragging involved. In sledding and in life, I realized I would rather walk up the hill by myself, covered in snow, than be mercilessly dragged behind. In the end,

I would be standing on my own two feet, ready to do beautiful things with my life.

I have learned precious lessons about when to hold on and when to let go. Truthfully, I am glad I held on to my marriage for as long as I did, because for 13 years it gave my children a father and a mother in their home. And in those 13 years, there were many good times that I am glad we didn't miss. Holding on also taught me that I am strong and that I fight for the things I value. Even when life is difficult, I now know God can depend on me to stand firm for what I believe in.

But perhaps the greatest benefit of holding on as long as I did was that when it came time to finally let go, I could do so with a clear conscience. All those years of hanging on allowed me to prove to myself and to the Lord that I was willing to do all He asked of me. I still have regrets about my marriage ending, but enduring so long gave me a blessed assurance that I did everything I could to make my marriage work. With that knowledge, my mind and heart are at peace.

Learning to let go is akin to the Serenity Prayer:

> God give me the strength to hold on to some things,
> the wisdom to let go of others things,
> and the courage to know the difference.

I learned to hold onto values, not to another person. I still believe marriage is honorable and worthy of our finest efforts. I support my friends and family in their marriages, but I have let go of the notion that I can force that value upon my husband or anyone else.

It may be that letting go of my husband helped me see my situation more clearly, or perhaps seeing my situation more clearly helped me let go of my husband. Either way, I realized that what I had always thought was tenacity on my part was a futile attempt to keep my husband in a marriage that he did not want. It was my valiant but doomed attempt to accept responsibility for his choices. Heavenly Father's plan hinges on agency and personal accountability, not forcing others to do the right thing. Once I let go of my husband, we were both free to make our own decisions and accept the consequences. Learning to hold on and to let go at the appropriate times has brought me the peace that comes from following God's Plan of Happiness—and that is a wonderful tradition, too.

24

My Exodus, My Art, My Salvation

My personal exodus out of my marriage began one very bad night when I came upon heartbreaking proof of my husband's numerous infidelities. I was overwhelmed with sickening evidence on our home computer of dehumanizing pornography and affairs. I even found his personal profile posted on a dating website—using a cropped photo that at one time had included me, no less! The caption on his profile read, "Single person looking for love." In that moment, my world changed forever. My life would never be the same. I would never be the same. But the silver lining of my story is that despite the heartache and distress, I do not regret going through this experience. The ways it changed me and my life for the better have been a blessing in disguise.

Of course, at the time of my discovery, I wasn't exactly counting my blessings. In fact, after uncovering all of the dirty secrets that lay hidden in our computer, I literally pushed it (and it was large!) onto the front lawn and, in a state of adrenaline-pumping rage, took a hammer to it until I had bashed it into tiny pieces. Yes, I admittedly lost it! I then went inside and proceeded to throw every last belonging my husband owned onto the front lawn. Looking back, it probably looked like a scene from a movie;

but in my hurt and disgust, I just couldn't be around anything that reminded me of him.

My only thought was, "How could he do this?" He had been living a double life right under my nose, and somehow I hadn't seen any of it. How could that be? Maybe the clues were there all along and I did not want to see them. All I knew now was that my husband was a total stranger to me. I didn't know this version of him nor did I want to. Having glimpsed the world he chose to live in, I couldn't help but feel repulsed. In my shock I did not know how to accept this as my new reality. It was not a dream, it was not even a nightmare. This was actually my life! The only thing I knew for sure was that our marriage was over.

I continued to learn more and more about my husband's unfaithfulness. After word of my divorce got out, a co-worker divulged to me that my husband had hit on her several times and had repeatedly attempted to start a relationship with her. To her credit, she had the integrity and respect for our friendship and my marriage to turn my husband down flat each time. In an odd way, I felt less crazy knowing that someone else knew what he was like. When I confronted him about my co-worker's allegations, my husband did not deny it, but he didn't seem to regret it, either. I felt everything from shock and disbelief to anger, sadness, and loneliness. I didn't know what my husband felt, if anything. We tried counseling a few times, but my husband was not at all interested in repairing our marriage or owning his infidelities. When only one marriage partner is willing and desires to repair the marriage, there is no chance of survival. It didn't take long to realize that my marriage was dead in the water. We separated, sold our home as part of our settlement, and finalized the divorce about a year later.

I now had to rebuild my life on my own. When marriage counseling didn't work, I had sought counseling for myself, which was a great help. But now I had decisions to make—hard decisions. Over the next several months, I slowly absorbed the trauma. Learning that the person I had loved and devoted my life to had so willingly betrayed me was a bitter pill to swallow. It left me with no capacity to trust and an overwhelming fear of being alone. I was terrified and very lonely. The two questions staring me in the face were now, "What am I going to do?" and "How am I going to survive alone?"

The next phases of my life, while difficult, brought incredible growth and blessings. One came from rediscovering a long-lost passion for art, and one came in the form of real-life angels who showered me with compassion and support when I needed it most. This is a tribute to both.

My Art, My Salvation

I have always been artistic, but somehow during my marriage I lost touch with that part of myself. I put most of my creative abilities into my marriage and very little back into myself. That turned out to be a mistake. By the time our marriage was over, I was so far out of balance I had almost forgotten my gifts and talents. I realized that in order to help myself, I had to create something bigger than myself.

My art gave me the means to do this. With a lot of hard work I became the artist I had always wanted to be and deep down knew I could be. Whether I am painting, sculpting, sewing, or assembling random objects, creating beauty brings me peace and helps me feel alive and happy again. I learned how to take my emotions - anger, pain, sadness, and even joy—and turn them into something meaningful through my art.

Becoming an artist did not happen overnight. I first had to turn inward, spending time completely alone with myself to remember who I was before the divorce and to get to know who I was going to be now, after the divorce. I then explored my craft from every angle I could imagine. I studied different types of art, went back to college, attended workshops and seminars, developed new friendships with other artists, and traveled to different cites and countries to observe art. I dedicated myself and my time to my new life's work. In artistic terms, you could say I sculpted a whole new world for myself.

Art allowed me to transform the sorrow of being alone into a blessing of emotional space that helped me develop my gift. The inner strength I had been searching for was finally accessible through developing my talent. My art allowed me to regain the self-confidence that had been so harshly beaten down through my divorce. I can now serve and reach out to others in a way that I never could in my marriage.

I continue to perfect my work, and I am now at a point where I am enjoying the fruits of my labors and using my talents to bless others as much as I can. I recently joined with other artists in selling our art to raise college scholarship money for underprivileged youth who are pursuing a degree in the arts. It is so rewarding to be able to give back in this way.

My art has also allowed me to connect more deeply with myself and those around me. During one of my art exhibits, a young woman approached me to compliment my work. She expressed her desire to be an artist. We talked about our lives and circumstances, and I learned that she was emerging from a recent and bitter divorce that had left her with serious health problems including a stroke and a condition that required major surgery—and she was only in her thirties! As I listened to her, I could literally feel what she was going through. I knew from my own experience the impact that stress from divorce can have on one's health. I tried to think of something that might bring her comfort and hope in the early stages of this trauma. The one thing I knew she needed to know was that she would indeed survive this. I assured her that if she had faith in herself, worked to find what she loved to do, and then pursued it, then she would come out on top. That is truth.

After she left the exhibit I could not hold back the tears. I was touched by her story, but it was more than that: in her I could see my former self. Just four years ago I had been her. Maybe I had forgotten how low I had truly been, or maybe I just didn't realize how far I had come over the years. But seeing my reflection in this woman's life allowed me to see the miracles that have been worked in my life. It was humbling and gratifying to say the least.

Getting through my divorce and finding my passion have been spiritual journeys for me. Once I learned to let go and let God guide me, I was able to find the "on" button for my talent. I now realized that God knew me better than I knew myself, and I trusted Him to guide me to the path I needed to be on. If I had resisted his help, I would have stayed stuck in my misery, never developing my art and missing out on opportunities to help others. It is difficult to see at the time, but when you're going through a major change like divorce (especially when you have little control or influence in the matter), it is helpful to remember that "what we resist will persist." It is better to surrender to the change and make the best of it. Now, after I have done everything I can do, I turn the rest over to God. In due season, the doors that are meant for me to go through will open, and I will continue to blossom artistically and spiritually.

Compassion Everywhere

My art was one mode of salvation through my divorce. The other was compassion. The time after my divorce was one of rebuilding. Forging my new life as a single woman was a struggle but would have been much harder if not for the real-life angels who literally came to my rescue. They came from Florida to California, some more unlikely than others, and all serving different purposes. But I am grateful that I kept myself open to their kindness, or I wouldn't have been able to recognize them. Thankfully, during my hardest times, I found compassion everywhere around me!

During my separation, a friend from work helped me move out of my house—an emotional experience to say the least. Not only that, she welcomed me into her home and insisted that I live with her and her family while I worked through this transition. What a healing experience this was for me. From her I learned so many things that allowed me to regroup from my losses and regain focus to move forward with my life. I learned from my friend's example how to be strong and confident and how to stand up for what is right. I felt inspired by her strength and faith. I wanted to be like her. She was not only a friend when I needed one, but also a role model and the stick of dynamite I needed to jump-start me into my new life. Thanks to her, the deep, dark hole I had been stuck in was now getting farther and farther behind me.

After a few months, I moved out of my angel friend's home and purchased a home of my own. What an exhilarating accomplishment this was! I felt so good knowing that I was becoming an independent, self-sufficient person. I started to see that I did in fact have the inner strength and faith to believe in myself and take care of myself. Occasionally, loneliness sets in, but I have learned to take a step back and remember that I am never alone as long as I have faith in the higher power that exists within me. Learning to trust myself helped me overcome my fears and lack of trust for others. I chose to be a survivor and decided I would live the best life I could create for myself.

Compassion came from many sources, but one of the most surprising came in an unexpected bond with one of my husband's mistresses. After following up on a suspicious phone number in Florida to which my husband had placed a stream of calls, I developed a surprisingly sweet relationship with a kind woman who, as it turned out, knew nothing of me and our marriage. She had been as much in the dark about me as I had been about her. Both feeling betrayed and exploited by the same man, we found in each other compassionate understanding that helped to heal our broken hearts. We were angels for one another.

Another person lovingly placed in my life at the right time was a male co-worker, who was also going through a divorce. His personal heartache made him keenly sensitive to mine, and that translated to kindness and understanding that were like balms to my wounds. From him I learned the importance of using our trials to help those suffering the same things.

Another life saver who appeared in my life just when I needed him most was a counselor from my husband's military base. Interestingly, I never met him in person; but through phone conversations and email, he gave me much-needed answers, advice, and encouragement. Even without knowing me, he believed in me. He encouraged me to start searching within myself to discover my passions and gifts. I had never had anyone offer me so much support and direction purely for my benefit. It felt wonderful!

Because of his influence and belief in me, I began the soul searching that lead me to return to my art. The counselor assured me that if I discovered and pursued my true passion, I would begin living an authentic and satisfying life. I followed his advice and, obviously, he was right!

I learned many important things from each person who showed me compassion in my time of need. From the two gentlemen who supported me, I was reminded that many men are honorable, moral, and kind. They were my advocates, guides, and friends when I was lost. From the woman in Florida, I learned not to place judgment. She turned out to be as much a victim in our situation as I was. I learned that women need each other and that we have a great deal of love and support to offer one another if we will stay open to each other. I also learned of the power of compassion to comfort and heal in a time when little else helps. The feeling of being cared about can make all the difference when taking those first shaky but hopeful steps and moving forward with a new life.

25

If You're Going Through Hell, Keep on Going

"If you are going through hell, keep going."
—*Winston Churchill*

One fateful afternoon, I found myself in a quiet corner of my favorite stationery store, simultaneously laughing and crying. I gazed in astonishment at the words in front of me. The pragmatic simplicity of the quote struck a chord: it was so poignantly me.

The months leading up to this moment had been filled with an excruciating pain that can only be described as Hell. But in this moment, reading this message, a hibernating personality within me awakened. My "Polly Positive" persona of days gone by quipped unapologetically, "Hey! Why on earth are you stopping here? If you don't like it in Hell, why are you sticking around? Keep Going!"

I had not laughed in months but suddenly found myself laughing out loud. As I did, my tears of sorrow turned into tears of hope, joy, and exhilaration. Those words were just the medicine I needed, and I determined then and there to remove myself from the endlessly spinning hamster wheel in my mind: an exercise that consumed much of my precious time and energy but that was getting me nowhere. I gave myself permission to get the heck out of Hell!

With a deluge of tears streaming down my face, I approached the check-out counter, red-eyed and sniffling, chuckling and gleeful—an utter contradiction to the perplexed cashier to say the least. But I did not care what she thought. I handed her my purchase: a shiny black refrigerator magnet with white-spiraled lettering immortalizing these wise words of Winston Churchill. It remains on my refrigerator to this day.

What brought me to that momentous day in the stationery store was one very bad choice followed by more than one very painful consequence.

On December 19, 2004, I was a divorced, thirty-eight-year-old, churchgoer and mother of two exceptional teen-aged boys. I was in great health and had several exciting business opportunities that were about to take flight. And I had a wonderful boyfriend who I believed loved me and wanted to marry me.

The next day, December 20, 2004, everything changed in an instant. I stepped into a public bathroom stall at the Crystal Court in the South Coast Plaza, took a test, and waited as the positive result slowly became visible. "Pregnant." For what seemed like an eternity I waited for the word "not" to appear in front. But it never came.

No! No! I heard my inner voice shout, the sound reverberating in my mind. I felt as though my soul had imploded within my body. My nausea increased tenfold, and I could scarcely stand. As I stood in shock, the Spirit spoke to my mind in a calm, clear, and distinct voice, saying just six words: "Everything is going to be okay."

"Oh, really," I shot back, "Everything is going to be okay? My entire life has just crumbled, and you are telling me that everything is going to be okay? Brilliant."

With no feeling in my legs, I somehow made my way to the bathroom mirror, which spanned the full length of the wall opposite from me. There was no escaping the view of my reflection. I saw my image and realized that the woman I had known as Kate was no longer. She was gone and was never coming back. I couldn't help asking, as I looked at this new person in the mirror, "Who are you?" This question would become my mantra over the next several months. *Who am I?*

I asked this question before every decision, before every action, before I rose up in the morning and before I went to sleep at night. Six days after my "discovery," on December 26th, 2004, the world watched as a tsunami wreaked cataclysmic destruction in Thailand. Fresh off my personal tsunami six days earlier, I understood pain in a new way and grieved for their loss more deeply. But with this understanding came a glimpse of perspective, the answer to my haunting question: *I am a daughter of God.* This simple but profound answer restored my hope and kept me grounded through the months to come. I knew unequivocally that I was a daughter of God, that he mourned with me, that he was aware of my situation, and that he would help me find the way. All I had to do was to be humble, teachable, and willing to do his will.

This knowledge made my journey possible but not easy. I was still mortified with debilitating shame and nearly paralyzed with fear that the formerly fearless Kate had never known. And to add insult to injury, the only other person who knew what was happening chose to abandon me entirely, leaving me on my own to deal with the aftermath. My boyfriend exercised his option to disappear, saying essentially that while he had "loving feelings" for me, he did not want to marry me. This situation was more than he could handle. I was bitter at the fact that he could walk away with such ease and leave me to face the consequences alone. I couldn't help but fantasize about how appealing such a disappearing act would be, but the reality was that I had two sons who needed me. Like it or not, this issue was going to be all mine.

Marriage and my dream of happily ever after would not be my fate. Late one night, alone in my room, I begged, pleaded, and bargained with my Father in Heaven to make this feeling and situation go away. I had never known this degree of desperation. My sins had left me with consequences that were inescapable, and the entire world would soon know what I had done. In truth, however, it was not what the world would think that concerned me most—it was what my children would think of me. How would this affect them? My transgressions were not only going to hurt me, they were going to have a long-lasting impact on my children and everyone dear to me. My life and theirs would never be the same again.

For two months, the loneliness and misery were exquisitely painful. My daily routine was as follows: I got my family off to school, carefully guarding my shameful secret. Then I would spend about two hours lying lifelessly in the fetal position on the floor of my tiny shower, hot water streaming onto my body, listening for the Lord's answers to my prayers. I sobbed until I had no more tears remaining. Exhausted and weak with morning sickness (or, for me, all-day sickness), I could not even get myself together for work. My entire future seemed dark and doomed. And if things weren't bad enough, the time was fast approaching to begin letting people in on my secret.

One night, I had fallen asleep on the sofa with the television turned on. I woke up at 2:30 A.M. to an Oprah Winfrey episode featuring women who had committed serious crimes who were now trying to come clean and turn their lives around. Despite their truly bad choices, the women seemed sincerely contrite and penitent. They were mothers and wives. Some of them had religious backgrounds. I listened intently to how they confessed to their families and communities and dealt with the various reactions— rejection, gossip, judgment—that swirled around them. The message that gave me hope was the promise that the people who love you and care about you will be there for you no matter what. People who truly know you will understand that you made some mistakes and that you are sincerely doing what you can to make amends. I started to believe that this would be the case for me, and it gave me the strength and courage I needed to tell my secret.

Having had nearly four months to prepare, I had rehearsed in my mind on a daily basis how the scenario would play out. I even strategized responses for all of the possible reactions my audience might have. I began telling my story to a few key family members first. My parents handled it well. My mother was so pleased that it wasn't cancer. I loved her at that moment for expecting something life-threatening; it made the impact of my message far less turbulent. How grateful I was that I had parents grounded in the gospel who lived life with an eternal perspective.

I went on to share my news with my brother and a few select friends who unknowingly opened the door of communication for me as though it had been scripted. I knew when that happened that it was God's way of telling me it was safe to trust this person. This was just one of so many tender mercies during this period of my life. The Lord always gave me just what I needed.

The disclosure I dreaded most, however, was telling my sons. My boys were 13 and 14 at the time. I planned to tell them after church one day. My younger son had brought up something during church that would give me the perfect segue. I rehearsed the intro to my speech in my head as we drove home, feeling more nauseous every minute. I knew that my children would never see me in the same light again. I also knew that I was about to complicate their already difficult teenage lives. They had already unfairly suffered the pains of divorce, and now, when they needed stability the most, their anchor had come loose from its mooring. How would I tell them that their straight-arrow mother who doesn't even watch R-rated movies had become pregnant out of wedlock? There is no way to prepare for such a moment. Nothing was more painful for me as a mother than knowing that I was inflicting deep wounds onto my innocent children. I knew that what I was about to tell them would have a deep and far-reaching impact on their lives, and I knew that the healing process for them and our family was not going to be quick or easy.

While that was all true, my children amazed me that day. It was a tearful exchange. I watched my thirteen-year-old as he sat silent, with long loose locks of hair covering his face and tears streaming down his cheeks. My fourteen-year-old, who is usually the least talkative regarding family matters, took a pragmatic and inquisitive approach. He asked direct questions and wanted real answers. I was astonished by their ability to comprehend the seriousness of the matter but also their ability to put aside their own feelings in order to see the bigger picture. They truly rose to the occasion although it was not without sorrow and disappointment. The price I paid was in realizing how much of their stability had rested in their feeling that they knew their mother. Before that day, I had been their rock, their go-to, their constant. Now they felt as though they didn't really know me. My heart broke at having let them down.

Personal responsibility is not an easy lesson. It is not easy to admit weakness and fault. I knew we could all be healed through the Atonement of Christ, but it was going to require a lot of work and faith. How could I be a shining example when I had sinned so seriously? How would I care for their needs as they dealt with difficult adult matters at such tender ages? How could I convince them of my broken heart and contrite spirit? How could I regain authority and respect in their eyes? How could I spare them embarrassment from my actions? Trying to imagine what they were experiencing was unfathomable. There was so much at stake. So much to undo.

I did have a plan, and I knew the plan was right, although it was not going to be without pain and sorrow for everyone involved. I had known since the week after learning I was pregnant that I was carrying a girl and that her name was Madison. My impressions of her were so strong that at times I felt her eager spirit cheering me on, lightly chiding, "Like it or not I am coming. Get used to it!" The veil felt very thin, and that was such a comfort to me. I knew that she knew me, loved me, and trusted me. I also knew that Madison was not to be ours. She had a family that was praying for her, and she was going to help me find them.

One night in bed, I felt an overwhelming sense of another woman's pain and longing. Someone else out there was hurting as much if not more than I was. I wondered if perhaps she could feel my sadness, too. At that moment, my self-pity gave way to a tremendous feeling of compassion and love for this woman that I had never met. I realized that pain is part of the package of this life, but suffering is a choice.

I began to choose to be grateful for my amazing body that had never experienced miscarriage, fertility problems, or serious health problems. I was now able to be grateful that I would take part in bringing this very special spirit into the world. My friend that I had never met would now have the opportunity to have her daughter through me. For some reason, this beautiful baby and our Father in Heaven were going to allow me to be a part of it. From that moment on, my mission was to find that family. I knew that my Father in Heaven would guide me.

As time progressed, I grew exponentially in my relationship with the Lord. I worked daily for inspiration and guidance from the Spirit. I learned quickly what it meant to grasp firmly to the word of God. It was my only lifeline. My understanding of the healing power of the Atonement took on a dimension and depth I had not experienced before. I knew that my sins could be forgiven; however, prior to this, I had not considered that my pain and devastation could also be healed and turned into great joy.

I had never presumed I could love and forgive in such a capacity. Our family experienced so many tender mercies and miracles. This period of gestation gave birth to an understanding of life and a love for Christ that I could have never gained otherwise. It took constant and diligent obedience to hear the Spirit guide me during that time, but I was blessed with many miracles and kindnesses in return. My sons were brave beyond measure. They sacrificed their own wants and feelings for the good of this precious sister that would leave our home after she was born. It was not easy for them, and they still feel that pain today.

My prayer is that the lessons learned during this period of their lives will one day shine in their hearts in a positive light. Healing often takes time and maturing, and they are still in their season of healing. But the Lord knows each of us intimately. He knows how to teach his children, how to show them his love and power. Patience, love, compassion, faith, forgiveness, hope unfailing, and charity are the paving stones that form the pathway to eternity.

Nearly six years have passed since that momentous day. Looking back, it is still arguably the worst day of my life. I will never be the same person that walked into that bathroom stall on December 20, 2004. But hopefully, in many ways I am better. How grateful I am to have a Savior and Father in Heaven that love me so much. They allowed me to grow in understanding and wisdom in such a miraculous manner, in spite of myself. They knew what I needed. They knew what I could become. They knew what was best for my family, for my dear angel Madison, and for her magnificent family.

The night I placed Baby Madison into the arms of her family was an experience like none other. When I felt as though my heart would stop beating, I felt it expand and grow within my chest. My capacity to love grew so much that my heart could not possibly break; it just got bigger. Our Heavenly Father does not take consequences away; however, if we allow it, He will make us stronger, give us the ability to bear the load with His help, and ultimately become more than we were.

Because of the atoning sacrifice of our Savior, I was able to be present in the sealing room of the San Diego Temple when Madison was sealed to her eternal family. Four years later, I was present again in that same temple as Madison and her family had another child sealed to them.

I know that when one door closes, several more open. It is up to us to find the open door. If we are true and faithful, our Father in Heaven will always be there to guide us. If we leave our hearts open to Him and His influence, we will not be deceived. I know this to be true.

The Lord is there to teach us how to make the worst days become our best growth opportunities. I can look back now and attest to the fact that sometimes the best happily ever afters do not happen as we might choose. Fortunately, however, the Lord has a way of creating something much grander out of our lives, and even our mistakes, than we could ever imagine.

26

Rocks, Rose Petals, or Empty Pockets

5 talents to one, 2 to another, and 1 for the third.
Talents were measures of worth in that day,
But who is to determine the weight or the worth?
Are trials sown treasures waiting to be reaped?

Of the one given 5, he returned with 5 more.
Of the one given two, he doubled his score.
Of the third so afraid, who buried his one,
It was taken away, and now he has none.

So what of our trials,
Afflictions and pain?
Have we reaped where sown
And returned with the gain?

A harvest of wisdom and knowledge to share,
Or did we bury in fear
The affliction and pain
We thought not to bear?

Will we carry the weight
In our pockets as rocks?
Turn away from His word,
And hide from our most worrisome parts?

Or will we gather rose petals
Of hope, gratitude and trust
That lighten, gladden,
And comfort our hearts?

Prayers of thanksgiving and praise
Double the worth of the most troublesome days.
Do not shrink from the task; bury it away,
Only to offer up empty pockets at that great day.

For one there are 5.
For you there are 2.
For the third there is one,
What will you do?

Will you offer
Rocks,
Rose petals, or
Empty pockets?

27

New Life in the Briar Patch

One of my favorite children's stories is the feud between Brer Fox (Brer meaning "brother") and Brer Rabbit. Brer Rabbit gets his paws stuck in a tar baby, the sticky trap set by Brer Fox. Brer Fox brags about how to finish off Brer Rabbit by hanging him from the highest tree or cooking him in the hottest oil. Brer Rabbit responds, "Hang me from the highest tree, or boil me in the hottest oil. But please don't throw me in the briar patch!" Finally, Brer Fox decides that if Brer Rabbit is most afraid of the briar patch, that is just where he is going to throw him. Brer Rabbit goes sailing through the air and disappears into the sticky, prickly bush of briars. Not long afterwards, Brer Rabbit emerges on a log looking as happy as can be, picking the tar out of his fur. He hollers to the astonished fox, "I was born and bred in the briar patch." The mess of twisted thorns was his home.

The unraveling of my marriage felt a lot like being thrown into the briar patch—but more in the sense of being tossed into a bed of thorns. It certainly didn't feel like home. My time in the briar patch was truly awful, the darkest period of my life. But to my astonishment, just like Brer Rabbit I survived and thrived in the briar patch. Some of you reading this understand all too well what

I mean, because you have been thrown into your own briar patch. You may still be wrestling to get free from the thorns. Maybe you are out of the briar patch now but still nursing your wounds. Or perhaps your time in the briar patch is only a memory marked by a well-healed scar. Wherever you are in your journey, I hope you can find hope and reassurance from my story.

My twenty-year marriage to my now ex-husband began full of love. I was living my dream of being a wife and mother. Unfortunately, as time went by, how my marriage looked from the outside was starkly different from what it was like on the inside. My husband was excessively harsh; and over time I went from being a vibrant and healthy person to a woman suffering from serious depression and anxiety. My weak interpersonal boundaries only made matters worse. With all my heart I wanted to be the kind of wife my husband wanted. Sadly, I could not satisfy his demands, and he began looking elsewhere. Presumably, to make life easier for him, he sent me out of state, hundreds of miles from home, to "work on my issues" with a psychologist. This was my first terrifying ejection into the briar patch. I found myself alone without my support system, away from my children, and in an area where I had had some traumatic experiences as a child. I was forced to go but not allowed to tell anyone where I was. I was forbidden from having contact with anyone from home while I was away. I suppose the point was to drive me over the edge of no return.

My friends and family protested the move, but my husband threatened me with divorce if I did not do as he requested; so I left my beautiful home with one suitcase to my name and moved into my new life in a small barren apartment with a mattress on the floor. I did it in hopes of saving the marriage. I told myself it would just be for a couple of weeks. I was wrong.

Safety in the Briar Patch

How do you begin to survive in the briar patch? Most nights I slept little. I worried unceasingly for my children and distressed over my circumstances. To cope, I turned to the only one on duty at 3:00 A.M.: the Lord. I needed to know He understood my broken heart and my outrageous situation. I needed to know He knew me.

Through bleary eyes I searched the scriptures and felt understood. Circumstances differed, but others had indeed experienced the same feelings I felt.

> Turn thee unto me, and have mercy upon me; for I am desolate and afflicted. The troubles of my heart are enlarged: O bring thou me out of my distresses. Look upon mine affliction and my pain. . . . O keep my soul, and deliver me: let me not be ashamed; for I put my trust in thee. Let integrity and uprightness preserve me; for I wait on thee. (Psalms 25:17–21)

Comfort came in those midnight hours with promises that spoke directly to me: "Thou shalt be far from oppression; for thou shalt not fear; and from terror; for it shall not come near thee" (Isaiah 54:14).

I realized that my little apartment was actually an escape from my oppression. The briar patch that first felt like thorns turned out to offer me safety.

My life transformed in the briar patch. I worked hard in therapy; but even without medication, my depression lifted in the first two weeks merely from being away from my husband's harsh treatment. That was the first of many miracles I experienced. I finally achieved real healing from the difficult experiences of my childhood. I lost the extra weight I had put on from previous trials of antidepressant medication. I found solace from attending the temple several times a week. The sweet spirit of revelation whispered frequently through the scriptures as I pondered in the quiet beauty of the temple.

My apartment was also going through a positive transformation. Between a kind new friend and the thrift store, I began to furnish and beautify my surroundings. At last, my children and husband were coming out for a visit; and I was so excited to show them a happier, more energetic and slender wife and mother. I couldn't wait for them to see my progress and help me pack to return home. But my husband was not pleased with my progress. He seemed surprised that I was weathering the separation rather than withering. He wanted me to stay away longer. My children clung to me during another tearful parting.

Rumors and Reliance on the Lord

Rumors at home abounded that I was "lazy in therapy" and "getting sicker and sicker," that I never really wanted to be a mother, and that I had abandoned my children for a career. Other women may have handled things differently, stood up for themselves, and spoken out more. Looking back, I wish I could have. I did the best I could with the resources I had at the time. Ultimately, it was a lesson for me that the Lord would work with me just as I was, love me, and guide me. He knows us perfectly and knows how to help us grow and find happiness.

Still, I was devastated by the rumors. It was so far from the truth; but with no word from me, what else could family, friends, and church leaders believe? Brer Rabbit's black sticky tar was all over me, and I could not shake my maligned reputation.

I felt helpless. My world felt foreign and unpredictable. Again I took comfort in scriptures that gave voice to my turmoil: "False witnesses are risen up against me, and such as breathe out cruelty . . . Wait on the Lord: be of good courage, and he shall strengthen thine heart: wait I say, on the Lord" (Psalms 27:12, 14).

I felt His assurance that He had everything in His hands and that my heart could have confidence in Him. In unforeseeable ways He offered me a life where the pain of rumors and rejection could be healed through His Atonement. This began a life of discipleship I had never envisioned. Feeling such personal assurances from the Lord began to build my relationship with Him in ways that I had never felt before.

New Life in the Briar Patch 161

Finding My Worth

Weeks turned into months, and my husband would not let me come home. He convinced me that I was too sick to come home but well enough to get a job to help with expenses. I complied, holding out hope that by cooperating he would let us be a family again. I still struggled to make decisions independently and stand up for myself.

Looking for work was a scary proposition. I had been a stay-at-home mom for 18 years. Even though I had an advanced degree, I felt worthless and believed no one would hire me. I proved myself right. I applied for a variety of odd jobs, from weeding in a nursery to cleaning horse stalls to bookkeeping. All with no success. Why wasn't the Lord helping me?

It turned out He was. I soon realized that certain doors closed so that I could walk through others the Lord had in mind for me—doors I didn't think I was capable of opening. I finally summoned the courage to apply for my dream job: a college instructor. I reconnected with a friend and cohort from twenty years ago who was now chair of the department. She knew my teaching and hired me part-time! Had my timing been any later, I would have missed her tenure as chair. It was a miracle.

The Lord was letting me know I was worth something. I started to see myself as He saw me: a valuable and capable daughter. Teaching reminded me of myself before the depression, before my low esteem. I was caught up in the cheerful delirium of students excited and engaged in learning. Faculty members enveloped me in a community where we shared our thirst for knowledge and love for teaching. The Lord had turned the briar patch into a greenhouse. There, he tutored me and carefully supplied experiences that helped me see myself as He saw me.

Trusting the Unexpected Answer

Although the briar patch grew more comfortable, my heart and family were still outside of it. I spoke daily with my children over the phone and felt their distress. It motivated me to drive hundreds of miles through the night to confront my husband. He agreed to marriage counseling but refused to take any responsibility for isolating me and made it clear that he had no intention to love, respect, or cherish me. Not exactly words that rebuilt my trust.

Prayer, fasting, and counseling with my church leaders lead to a clear directive: "Get out of the marriage immediately." It was not the answer I wanted nor did it seem possible that it could be right. There had to be a way to heal our marriage. We had made covenants. Wasn't marriage forever? The answer came again and again, each time with more strength and more urgency. My new relationship with the Lord gave me the courage to trust Him. I filed for divorce.

Bolted Doors and the Way Opened

It was difficult managing divorce court appearances in one state while teaching in another. I convinced myself this was temporary and thought I would soon be home taking care of my children. My husband had other plans. He bolted the doors to our house (which was still *our* house) and refused to let me come in or see my daughters. In one of the lowest moments of my life, he called the police, who searched my car for weapons and threatened to handcuff me in front of my neighbors. I was terrified and humiliated. They wouldn't let me get close to my daughter and wouldn't bother to verify my name on the deed to the house. I was even threatened with going to jail unless I agreed not to go to church at our family ward the next day. I wanted to melt into a puddle on the driveway. All I could think to do was to agree. My world had turned upside down. How could this be happening?

What my husband had done was not legal. A judge who was a friend of mine verified that, but it didn't change much. The people involved were not looking at the law. I felt like the Psalmist: "False witnesses did rise up; they laid to my charge things that I knew not. They rewarded me evil for good. . . . Lord, how long wilt thou look on? Rescue my soul from their destructions" (Psalms 34:11–12, 17).

I took comfort in King David's words and in knowing I was not the only one who had suffered false accusations. The Savior himself experienced it many times. The Lord not only sees our lives, but he also experiences them with us. His empathy is complete. He also knows exactly how to help us through it. He let me know through the scriptures that He was aware of my circumstances and was watching over me.

The Lord Has Custody of My Children

During our marriage, most of the encounters my children had with their father left them in tears; yet, surprisingly, he fought for full physical custody with no contact from me. He won. The court actually ruled for joint custody, giving the children the right to choose with whom to live, but I believe my children did not feel they had a real choice. They knew what was familiar. They did not know that the briar patch in which I lived could offer them safety and peace.

Bereft of my children, my heart was torn out of my chest. It was so physically painful I could hardly breathe. There would be no more heart-to-heart talks, no ballet recitals, no making their birthday cakes, no cheering them at choir concerts, no sewing their prom dresses, no making sure they took their medicine, and no comforting them when they were in the hospital. My children were deprived of their mother.

I pleaded with the Lord. My children needed me. I needed them. I did not understand how He could let us be separated. My only solace came from Isaiah: "All thy children shall be taught of the Lord; and great shall be the peace of thy children" (Isaiah 54:13).

This was the most difficult promise, but I have seen the literal fulfillment of this blessing over the years. At all times my heart was drawn out to Him for my children. I prayed earnestly and ceaselessly that people would be raised up to help my children in my stead: good women, role models, faithful friends, and worthy young men to date. Without contact, I could only imagine my children's day-to-day lives. But to my joy they seem to be making good choices. They are active church members, returned missionaries, college graduates, and spouses who have been married in the temple. Despite my loss, I believe a merciful Father fulfilled His promise, because they are His children, too.

Single Partnership with the Lord

Starting over single was such a lonely and uncertain time. How would I manage as a single woman? I had little confidence in my ability to make decisions. I often depended on priesthood blessings to guide me. One blessing directed me to lean on the Savior as I would a husband—to go to Him for council and abide in His love: "For thy Maker is thine husband; as a woman forsaken and grieved in spirit . . . with great mercies will I gather thee" (Isaiah 54: 5-8).

I learned there was no task too mundane to receive the Lord's help. Budgeting, car repairs, medical problems, anything. Eventually my confidence grew, and I was able to make larger and larger decisions, even purchasing a beautiful home on my own.

My Mourning Turned to Dancing

It was only by being thrown out of my toxic marriage and into the briar patch that I could find a new and healthy life. I learned about unhealthy relationships and how to identify the "crazy making." Several colleges hired me part-time. I got accepted to a Ph.D. program at a university ranked third in the nation (even when my brain had been academic mush for 18 years).

Blessings continued to pour in. I rediscovered my love for life, playing tennis, riding horses, the theater, being artistic, scuba diving, and serving others. I found sanctuary and guidance in the temple every week. Dear friends took me into their family, held my hand in court, and shared meals, birthdays, vacations, time, and hope. When I recently signed up for a ballet class, I realized the Lord had literally "turned for me my mourning into dancing" (Psalms 29:11).

A Heart to Know the Lord

Most importantly, I found a relationship with Christ. Not a sanctimonious, ivory tower Jesus, but the real, have-a-dialogue-with, help-me-survive-this-day, please-heal-my-heart Redeemer. In my religious upbringing I had been introduced to the Sunday School Christ, but I didn't really know Him. More than anything, I wanted the promise in Jeremiah 24:7: "I will give them a heart to know me, that I am the Lord."

I could not have had the heart to know my Savior had I not been stripped of my life outside the briar patch, had I not been shamed, blamed, ostracized, and forced to depend on Him in a way I had never depended on Him before. As many others have testified, it is in this lonely crucible that our life with Him is forged. I will never be the same.

Trust Him When I Am Snagged

Does this mean I am without struggles? No. My hope and faith weaken periodically. No briar patch is free from thorns. I still get snagged, and it is painful. Having had no contact with my children for the last nine years is the most painful thorn. They have lived so much of their lives without me. This part of my heart is still waiting on the Lord. How do I cope? Sometimes I feel that I will never be comforted. But other times I know that if He can rescue me from a marriage where my soul was dying, then He, as the divine "repairer of the breach," can deliver my children to me again (Isaiah 58:12). The more I see the Lord fulfill other promises in my life, the more I trust that the promise of a celestial family will be mine, too.

Good Tidings

God has a plan for each of us. It is hard to see it when we are covered in tar, sailing through the air and headed for a sticky, prickly briar patch. But as we sit on a log and pick the tar out of our fur, a whole new world appears. In this moment, we are home in a way we never dreamed of. What looked like a prison of thorns to break me actually freed me, healed me, and saved my life. This briar patch is now my treasured home. I find love, protection, and self-worth here. Who knows what else I might find?

> The Lord hath sent me to preach good tidings unto the meek; he hath sent me to bind up the brokenhearted, to proclaim liberty to the captives, and the opening of the prison to them that are bound. (Isaiah 61:1)

28

Heaven and Hell in the Hallway

You would think that growing up in the South would make me a country music lover. But I didn't become a fan until I filed for divorce. Maybe I was drawn to the down-home beat of the music, or maybe I just related to all that "lost my dog, lost my job, lost my home, lost my man" stuff. One particular verse caught my attention in a time when I needed the courage to keep moving: "If you're goin' through hell . . . keep on movin.'"

We all love the beginning of a story, full of promise: getting a new puppy, finding a great job, buying a new house, meeting the man of your dreams. And we love happy endings: the dog is trained, the job blossoms into a career, the house becomes a home, you marry your soul mate. Sadly, we don't live for long in the hopeful beginning or happy ending of the story. We live most of our lives in the in-between—the uncertain, often messy struggle to simply make it through.

A friend described it this way: "When God closes one door, he opens a window . . . but it's hell in the hallway." The hallway is the in-between. The dark, scary place where you don't know what is going to happen or how things will turn out. Many a soul has fainted in the hallway from loss of hope.

What brings us to the hallway varies. It could be losing your dog, your job, your home, or someone you love. In my story, I lost them all. It was the darkest hallway of my life. But mine is also a story of how I found the hope to "keep on movin'" until I found a window out of the hallway.

Talking about the hallway is a social risk. It is safer to talk about happy endings; but, this can keep us isolated and afraid when we need support and companionship the most. I sat alone in my dark hallway, too scared to ask for help or to share how insecure and terrified I felt. Fortunately for me, I found a friend in the hallway—a woman in my divorce support group who opened up about the pain of missing her children, the children her husband had taken away from her. To her surprise and mine, she was not alone in her plight. Woman after woman sighed in empathy and relief. We all thought we were the only one.

This profound realization that we had company in the hallway felt like someone had turned on a night light. We had each been stumbling around in the dark, ashamed to admit we could not find our way, then *bling!* A tiny glow. There were other women like ourselves: faithful, stalwart women who had been treated as if they were crazy, incapable, and not worthy of motherhood. We clung to each other and found strength in our shared faith and circumstance.

Our stories were so alike. Each time one of us talked about the hallway, the rest of us gave a collective sigh of relief. "He told our bishop I was taking our money, but in reality he was spending it on pornography." We nodded. Been there. "I've believed I was worthless for so long. Who will love me if I divorce him?" Heavy sigh. Been there, too. We traced the genealogy of our worthlessness like branches of a pedigree chart. It started with an unaffectionate parent, a cruel nickname at school, and finally an abusive marriage, until we arrived at our place in the hallway. And finally admitted it out loud.

As we groped for answers together, we found something astonishing: each other. And more women followed. Four women grew to seven, ten, then twelve. We found comfort, humor, and faith between the narrow walls of the hallway that gave us hope that we would each see sunlight again. We all celebrated when one of us reconnected with her children. Her victory was our victory and became hope for our own. This shared faith and strength only comes when we let people hear us breathing; when we talk about our hallways.

Faith Shaken: The Door Closes

My faith has always anchored my soul through hard times. I honor my church leaders. I look to them for inspiration and guidance. But when I finally had the courage to tell my church leaders about the problems in my marriage, they didn't believe me. Maybe they just couldn't believe that my husband, who looked close to perfect from the outside, could do what he did. Or maybe they just weren't prepared to deal with the severity of the consequences. So they advised me to go back to my husband. I had always followed the counsel of my church leaders; but in this instance, I felt misguided. The direction I felt from the Lord was to file for divorce. How could the two be so different? Who was wrong? Either option felt like a loss. Either option closed a door. Either option was going to shake my faith at its core. And either option propelled me into the hallway.

The Taboo: Stop Breathing

I would have given anything to know a woman who had gone through a similar experience. How did she make decisions? How did she come through it? Unfortunately, telling divorce stories at church felt taboo. It wasn't a common topic in church meetings or lessons. I am embarrassed to admit that before my divorce I considered divorced women to be on the periphery of church membership, their stories prompting a raised eyebrow or a hushed whisper. I was so ashamed to be in the divorce hallway that I didn't talk about it. I didn't know what to do or whom to go to for help. If my church leaders didn't believe me, would anyone else? Once you have been dismissed by family, friends, children, leaders, or someone to whom you turned for support, it is hard to allow yourself to trust again. I hope that my story assures you that you are not alone. There are those of us who have been through it and understand.

The Shame: Alone in the Dark

Although the courts awarded joint custody, my ex-husband prevented me from having contact with my children and cut off all communication with me. As a formerly stay-at-home mom, I couldn't imagine how my children would get through the divorce without my love and support. Surely a God who could part the Red Sea and turn water into wine could reconnect me with my young ones. I had never known of any mother who was forbidden to have contact with her children. Even mothers in prison get to see their children. I reeled with the shock and the shame. In addition to losing my husband, I had now lost my children. The hallway became darker and darker.

The Glimmer: The Crack of a Window

My glimmer of hope was that the Lord had not left me friendless. The friends and family members who stayed by my side and loved me through my darkest time were life savers. They heard my pain. They let me talk about the hallway. The Lord blessed them with unique experiences that enabled them to help me. I felt the Lord helping me through my friends; and gradually, I began to recognize the Lord in my life again. These friends stepped into the hallway with me. They arranged to be with me in the many court appearances, loaned me their car, hired me, fed me, comforted me, rescued photos of my children for me, and even helped to retrieve some of my belongings. These Christlike brothers and sisters in the Church restored my faith in priesthood leadership, sisterhood, and personal revelation.

Other hallway companions came from unlikely places. A seven-year-old boy living in the apartment above me reached out to me in the most surprising way. The son of a struggling single mother who didn't have much in the way of toys for himself spent his birthday money on a present for me: a soft, new teddy bear. When I thanked him and attempted to refuse his sweet gesture, he innocently suggested, "Maybe the bear could take the place of your husband."

Even beyond his selfless generosity, I was touched at this young boy's awareness of my loss and willingness to talk about something others considered taboo. Perhaps he had heard me cry myself to sleep at night through the thin apartment walls. Maybe he was all too familiar with this kind of pain, because he had seen it in his own mother. Either way, he saw my need and reached out to me. With his mother's permission I accepted this precious gift and treasure the bear still today. And even more, I treasure the hallway visit with my sweet, young friend.

The Light: The Son

As wonderful as these friends were, they couldn't be expected to be available 24 hours a day. Sleepless with grief, I often soaked my pillow with my tears. My scriptures became my best friend. I found in those sacred pages a story of someone who truly understood me and how it felt to be in the hallway. In Psalms 6:6 I read, "I am weary with my groanings; all the night make I my bed to swim; I water my couch with my tears."

Each passage was followed by a promise of comfort and assurance that the window would open. "And the Lord God will wipe away tears from off all faces" (Isaiah 25:8).

Between tearful episodes, I was now able to find joy in small things like the changing seasons or a cool sip of water. When I was scared about how I would pay my rent, I read: "I am in trouble: hear me speedily" (Psalms 69:17). "The Lord hath heard my supplication" (Psalms 6:9). "The Lord also will be a refuge for the oppressed, a refuge in times of trouble" (Psalms 9:9).

My new bishop offered temporal assistance to assure I had enough money for food and rent. This was not easy to accept, especially as I saw my ex-husband's material wealth increase after the divorce while mine decreased. My sense of injustice was assuaged as I read: "Fret not thyself, neither be thou envious. Trust in the Lord, and do good ...and verily thou shalt be fed. Delight thyself in the Lord; and he shall give thee the desires of thine heart" (Psalms 37: 1–16).

The Lord has met all my needs. I have plenty of food, clothes, and I have a good home. I am able to pay for my schooling; and I love what I do for a living. I am living a rich and blessed life.

When I yearned for my children to reconcile with me, I read, "The Lord bindeth up the breach of this people and healeth the stroke of their wound" (Isaiah 30:26). One day, I am assured, He will bind up our relationships, and we will be together again.

When I thought the sadness and grief of the hallway would last forever and my life would never get better I read: "For the Lord shall be thine everlasting light and the days of thy mourning shall be ended" (Isaiah 60:20).

Now my spirit is mending and the Lord is giving me "beauty for ashes, the oil of joy for mourning, the garment of praise for the spirit of heaviness" (Isaiah 61: 3).

I am moving through my hallway and finding the window He has opened to me.

The Talk: Breathe Out Loud

We *can* talk about the hallway while we are in it. We can start breathing out loud. It is the adversary and our own fears that make it taboo. Holding our breath until the proverbial window opens to our happy ending only isolates us during the process. We need to find each other and seek the light together.

My hallway is filled with wonderful people who give me faith in my happy ending and help me open my window wider and wider. I am no longer in the hallway by myself. This Southern girl may have stumbled on a new hit country song: "Party in the Hallway." Well, maybe not a party—but a little relief that can feel like heaven!

29

Where Do I Belong?

As it is for many, my divorce was dramatic and traumatic. I was overwhelmed by the flurry of life-changing decisions. But sometimes the trauma comes in small and ordinary experiences—the ones that happen every day and every week, reminding us that our life is forever changed and we will never be the same. Part of me said, "Good, I won't miss the pain and the daily put-downs." I do, however, miss knowing where I belong. At least I knew my place in that old relationship. I knew where to park my car, where to sit, and on which side of the bed to sleep. In this new life I didn't know where I belonged.

I compare it to the feeling of moving into a new home. You go to put your toothbrush away in the medicine cabinet and blindly reach left like you always did in the old house, only to find that in the new bathroom the medicine cabinet is on the right. It's a little thing, an ordinary daily task, but there is some unease, not knowing where the new toothbrush belongs. It opens up a whole new set of questions. Do I really want the brush to go in the medicine cabinet? What about putting it in a cup on the counter, instead? Or in the drawer? It is one small, disconcerting event; but multiply this by the hundreds of changes divorce brings, and the emotional strain can be overwhelming.

One such tension is the weekly quandary, "Where do I sit at church?" The first Sunday I went to church alone after my divorce, I didn't know where to sit. I walked through the back doors of the chapel and just stared at the rows of pews. Feelings of confusion, vulnerability, and aloneness almost propelled me to turn around and go home. Before the divorce, I had never thought about where to sit. When I was married I always had my children and husband to sit with. Now all the rules had changed. I was no longer looking for space for a family; I was just one person. I didn't need to find the end of the bench in the middle of the chapel like my husband preferred. I had to figure out what I preferred. I didn't know.

Walking down the aisle alone, I felt exposed and conspicuous. Could everyone see I was lost and wandering? Should I find an empty pew? Would anyone come and sit by me? What if they didn't? Could everyone tell I was alone? Perhaps I could just slide in next to a family so I didn't look like I was by myself. Maybe if I offered to help a mother with her wiggly children the family would let me sit by them. These questions only increased my anxiety. I reminded myself to breathe. How did such a molehill decision become a mountain?

I began to notice other single people scattered around the chapel, each an island sitting alone. Maybe they felt out of place, too. Each Sunday I coaxed myself to sit by someone new. I first sat by another single woman. With books and purse, she had built a fortress around herself. I couldn't even get close enough to share a hymn book with her. Next I sat by a single man. He thought I was coming on to him and excused himself to sit out in the foyer. I tried coming in late and sitting in the back so no one would notice me but couldn't hear the service for all the children also sitting in the back. I tried sitting in the front rows. I could hear, but the benches were bare, and I felt more conspicuous.

One Sunday, to my relief, I was assigned a place to sit, a place to belong. The bishop called me to be one of the church organists. Every other Sunday I had an assigned seat next to the organ. It gave me a legitimate reason to sit alone, without pressure to find a place in the congregation. Perhaps finding a seat should not have been such an ordeal, but it was.

Since sharing my seating dilemma with others, I have learned that numerous single church members echo my concerns. They laugh nervously as they recognize themselves in my silly, yet poignant, story. Single women feel vulnerable and isolated at a time in their lives when companionship and inclusiveness are critical. Single men have an even more complicated dilemma. Some worry that sitting by another man will be perceived as a same-gender attraction and that sitting by a female will be seen as a come-on. To sit by a family may be interpreted as an unhealthy interest in that family's children. To compensate, many default to sitting by themselves as far away from everyone else as possible, against the walls or in the back.

The solution my friends and I found to be most helpful was simply to get the issue out in the open. We discovered we weren't the only ones feeling awkward and alone. We felt understood. And most of all, we came up with a solution: we sit with each other, clusters of single women and men, friends in the same boat. We now smile knowingly as we find our seats together. There is a sigh of relief and a twinkle of humor as we collectively share this secret dilemma and transform it. When we have the courage to talk about our problems, no matter how silly they may seem, we can solve them together. The problem loses its power to humiliate and invoke fear once you know others are watching out for you. I am no longer the organist, but I barely miss a step now when I enter the chapel. I now see friends who welcome and make room for me on the pew.

I have since learned that single people are not the only ones who struggle with this issue. While speaking at a single adult training meeting for church priesthood leaders and their wives, I was surprised to learn that so many wives experienced the same awkwardness and loneliness in finding a seat in the chapel while their husbands sit on the stand. This had never occurred to me. I was so self-conscious about my own singleness that I was oblivious to others, single or married, going through the same thing.

My dilemma now has turned to one of choosing from all the people I could sit with: my single friends, a church leader's wife, a new couple on their first Sunday, a family trying to keep their children happy through the meeting, a teenager who seems to be struggling. I now see myself as not all that different from anyone else at church. At least no less valuable and needed. We are a family, a church family. We all bring something different, but we all belong. I now know there is a place for me when I walk into the chapel. And I know there are people like me hoping I will make a place for them.

30

Red Flags and Roses

My road to divorce began before I was married. Several red flags made their appearance early on in our courtship, but I chose to ignore them. Now I am a divorced mother. I could elaborate on many of the red flag lessons learned, but those are for another essay. This is instead a story about surviving heartbreak, enduring, and finding hope through the Atonement of Christ.

I guess you could say it took a bomb exploding in my marriage to force me to wake up to my reality. The day I received yellow roses and the other woman received red roses was the day the bomb went off. It was Valentine's Day, a holiday now marked with deep pain and sadness. I was married to my college sweetheart. We had grown up in the same neighborhood. Up until this point, I thought I knew him well. After a long courtship, we married.

Many long years of educational training and hard work afterwards were supposed to be worth the sacrifice. He became very successful in his field of training. I was a teacher, wife, and mother, and had been primarily responsible for holding down the fort for our family through the many years of school and training.

Being the wife of a post-graduate professional in training was a lonely life. I had known it would be, but not to such a great extent. During my husband's post-graduate training, the head of his program informed all of us married couples that the divorce rate for their school was very high. I was being too optimistic, but I honestly believed it could never happen to us. Our marriage would survive anything!

There were moments, however, when I felt the Spirit caution me that our marriage was in jeopardy. Looking back, I did not listen as closely as I should have. I had, in fact, noticed my husband growing more distant throughout the years. In truth, the Lord had been whispering to me since the beginning of our marriage that things were not right.

The scriptures tell us that we will know in our hearts and in our minds the truth of all things. Despite the Lord's attempts to warn me, I allowed my fear of the truth and fear of being more alone than I already was to hinder my faith. Fear and faith, I know now from personal experience, cannot exist together.

Still, we had come so far together. Best of all, we had our beautiful children. I had a very high-risk pregnancy—a rough time for us—but our baby was born healthy and strong. I had also suffered miscarriages, two of which occurred within two years of my husband leaving. The losses were devastating to me and even to our young children. We had seen our two babies and heard their heartbeats. They were strong right up until I somehow miscarried them. I was so sad. I felt very alone.

Shortly thereafter, we were ready to settle down and raise our family. We moved to a new home, new town, new everything. My husband's company was doing well. I was looking forward to building and enjoying life together with our family. That is, until the Valentine's Day surprise.

On Valentine's Day, I received a phone call from a stranger. He proceeded to tell me that my husband was seeing his girlfriend, who was also a co-worker. He divulged that this other woman had received red roses from my husband on Valentine's Day. As much as I didn't want to believe him, I knew in my heart he was telling the truth. I could deny it no longer.

The first few moments after hearing this kind of news were indescribable. I felt numb, stunned, speechless, in shock. "Not my husband!" is all I remember thinking, followed by a disheartening understanding, "No wonder my roses were yellow!" So much for my husband's claim that the out-of-town florist had made a mistake!

This was the bomb that blew apart our marriage. No more pretending, no more denial. Our family would never be the same again.

Within the hour I presented my husband with this new information. He admitted to the roses but denied any romantic relationship. I didn't buy it. It was time to be real. It is very difficult to work on saving your marriage, hoping for a second chance, with a third party involved.

I spent the next few weeks trying to make sense of what had become of our marriage. My husband and I made attempts at counseling, but it was not successful. The counselor, someone recommended by my husband and not of our faith, did not help us move toward reconciliation. It became apparent that our chances of mending our marriage were slim with only one of us willing to do the work and the third party stubbornly positioned between us.

Three weeks later, I came home with our children one evening after taking them to see the beautiful Broadway play, *Joseph and the Amazing Technicolor Dreamcoat,* to find that my husband had moved out while our children and I were at the show. With no warning and no discussion of his final decision to leave our family, he was simply gone. It was the single worst day of my life. I carried our children into their rooms. They were sound asleep, thank goodness. I then went to our bedroom, fell to the floor on my knees, and sobbed. All I could do was pray to the Lord in my desperation. He was there for me. I felt Him all around me— His warmth, His compassion, His mercy, His understanding, His unconditional love. I had never felt the Lord's love to that degree. In that darkest moment of my life, I was so grateful for it. That moment is forever vivid in my mind.

I don't think it was a coincidence that we had just come from seeing *Joseph and the Amazing Technicolor Dreamcoat*. I felt like Joseph did in the scene where he is in prison, singing the song, "Close Every Door." Everything had been taken away from Joseph, everything that mattered to him in his life. I felt his pain to the core. I knew that the Lord was there for me and our children, and He knew what we were about to go through. I believe that seeing this beautiful Broadway play that night was a sweet tender mercy from the Lord.

That night, I knew the Lord would be there for us as long as we reached out to Him. This was the greatest blessing my children and I received. We have never lost sight of it. I have a new appreciation for the pain and suffering that the Lord endured for each of us in the Garden of Gethsemane. I know from this experience that He knows me and my suffering and how to comfort and heal me. He became my best friend through this trial and continues to be my best, truest friend. One of the scriptures that brought me the greatest comfort is, "Be still and know that I am God." I am so grateful for the Atoning sacrifice that the Lord made for all of us.

That night as I kneeled on my knees, I made a promise to the Lord that I would always be there for our children no matter what. I knew He would help me. He always has, and still does to this day.

Our children and I moved back to our former hometown to start anew. I naively hoped my husband would join us, giving our family a chance to start over far away from the other woman. We had talked about the possibility. Contrary to my desire and our children's hopes and wishes, my husband said goodbye. Thankfully, I knew with the strongest assurance I have ever been blessed with that the Lord was directing our path. I would go back and raise our children with the peace and security of a loving family and true, forever friends around us.

This was a time of constant leaning on the Lord. Several times a day, I found myself on my knees seeking guidance, direction, and answers to my prayers. Many pant legs became worn at the knees. I came to love the scripture found in John 14: "Peace be with you, my peace I give unto you. Not as the world giveth, give I unto you." I also relied on the words of D&C 6:14–24, that in part say:

> Verily, verily I say unto you, blessed art thou for what thou has done; for thou hast inquired of me, and behold, as often as thou has inquired thou hast received instruction of my Spirit. If it had not been so, thou wouldst not have come to the place where thou art at this time . . . Yea, I tell thee, that thou mayest know that there is none else save God that knowest thy thoughts and the intents of thy heart.

These are just two of the many beautiful scriptures I loved and depended on to give me much added and needed strength through the years raising my children.

My husband rationalized his leaving by saying things like, "The children will be fine because they have you; kids are resilient," and, "I haven't loved you for the last seven years." The pieces of the puzzle were slowly coming together. I was beginning to see how my husband had gradually been growing more distant from me and our marriage for a long time.

This level of emotional disconnection doesn't happen overnight. It is a process, a long process. If we do not protect and take care of each other, little by little, our marriage will begin to grow weaker, opening the door for little mistakes that lead to bigger mistakes. Satan presents temptations slowly and persistently until he has finally convinced us that the only way we'll ever find real happiness is by getting out of the relationships that matter the most. The truest protection we can give to our marriage and our family is to put the Lord and one another first.

Our divorce was and still is the greatest heartache of my life. Satan won this battle. I wish I would have had the courage to address the promptings of the Spirit I'd had earlier on in our marriage. Perhaps if I had insisted on us going to counseling much earlier, things would have turned out differently. Then again, when I did bring up concerns back then, my husband blamed our emotional distance on his busy schedule. He would then promise me that things would get better once he finished. I had always hoped he was right.

I own the part I played in the unraveling of our marriage. I didn't use my voice. I let fear of accepting the truth of our disconnect, of feeling so alone in our marriage, overcome the faith that I should have had to address the void. Just maybe we could have had a second chance to save our marriage, our family. It was a heavy lesson I had to learn and accept.

We survived divorce, and our children are doing well. It was a long, hard road. Our divorce proceedings lasted years too long. Every "surprise" brought new levels of hurt, disappointment and sadness. But through this, our children and I stayed close to the Lord. We knew He would never leave us alone. The new home and life we rebuilt together became our special place, our sanctuary. We built strong testimonies and conviction of the Lord's unconditional love for us through these trials and experiences.

One of our treasured memories through the years that followed was reading and talking about the scriptures each night, then having family prayer. It was the most peaceful, tender, heavenly time for us each day. One that is very dear to us is 3 Nephi 17:20–24 where the Lord blesses the children:

> Blessed are ye because of your faith. And now behold, my joy is full. And when He said these things He wept, and he took their little children, one by one, and blessed them, and prayed unto the Father for them. And when He had done this He wept again; And He spake unto the multitude, and said unto them; Behold your little ones. And as they looked to behold they cast their eyes towards Heaven, and they saw the heavens open, and they saw angels descending out of heaven as it were in the midst of fire; and they came down and encircled those little ones about, and they were encircled about with fire; and the angels did minister unto them.

Through this scripture, we knew that the Lord would protect and encircle us with the warmth of His love.

One of the hardest challenges I have had to address is learning to trust again. The protective walls went up for both myself and our children. I knew this was a reasonable means of self-protection. I also knew that living with walls up is not what the Lord wants for us. It has become a matter of prayer with a lot of faith for me to work on overcoming my fears of being hurt again. Alma 32: 27 has been a great help:

> But behold, if ye will awake and arouse your faculties, even to an experiment upon my words, and exercise a particle of faith, yea, even if ye can no more than desire to believe, let this desire work in you, even until ye believe in a manner that ye can give place for a portion of my words.

Alma's encouragement to at least "desire to believe," even with only a particle of faith, gives me hope. Many times I could only take one step at a time, sometimes one minute at a time, putting one foot in front of the other with hope and believing. Faith over fear.

I would not wish divorce on anyone, ever. But the lessons I learned have made me stronger and wiser, because I let them. Life goes on; and if we let the Lord be our anchor and constant companion, we can weather the storm and pass the test. It is through our tests that we are stretched, pulled, and perfected in this life, as long as we remember that the Atonement of Jesus Christ is the source of all hope, love, and joy.

One scripture in particular has given me much strength through the years. Helaman 5:12 states:

> And now, my sons, remember, remember that it is upon the rock of our Redeemer, who is Christ, the Son of God, that ye must build your foundation; that when the devil shall send forth his mighty winds, yea, his shafts in the whirlwind, yea, when all his hail and his mighty storm shall beat upon you, it shall have no

power over you to drag you down to the gulf of misery and endless wo, because of the rock upon which ye are built, which is a sure foundation, a foundation whereon if men build they cannot fall.

I have realized that my ex-husband and I are both on this eternal journey together as parents of our wonderful sons and as children of God. The deep feelings I felt for my ex-husband haven't died; rather, my love for him has been transformed into a pure, Christlike love through the Atonement.

I have faith that no matter what life may bring us in the future, we can and will stand strong on the rock of our Savior. We will get through it all, always together, forever! For this I am grateful!

31

Thou Mayest

In John Steinbeck's novel, *East of Eden,* there is the most beautiful account of agency. We see the choices the characters have before them, the choices they make, and the ramifications of those choices. There is a particularly poignant part in the novel where three of the main characters discuss the Old Testament story of Cain and Abel. One line in the story reads, "Thou shalt." The three scholarly men trace these two words back to their Hebrew origin and discover that they translate to "Timshel," which means, "Thou mayest." Steinbeck goes on to write,

> Thou Mayest—that gives a choice. It might be the most important word in the world. That says the way is open. That throws it right back to man. For if Thou Mayest it is also true that Thou Mayest not. Thou Mayest! Why that makes a man great, that gives him stature . . . for in his weakness . . . he has still the great gift of choice. He can choose his course and fight it through and win. I have new love for that glittering instrument, the human soul. It is a lovely and unique thing in the universe. It is always attacked and never destroyed . . . because Thou Mayest." (pp. 301–2)

Agency! A gift I consider the greatest given to human beings. Agency allows us the opportunity to transcend, to adapt, and to evolve through life. Agency gives us the opportunity to become great. It is through our gift of agency that we can choose to be forgiving and loving. We can also, because of this great gift, choose to be judgmental and withhold forgiveness.

I suspect that many of us have tender stories of forgiveness. I am sure each of us can recount a time in our lives when love made a difference. The following is my story of that time: the opportunity I was given to learn forgiveness and the power of love.

Six years ago, my dad chose to take his own life. That night, my mom climbed onto her bed and patted my dad's pillow—the down pillow that still carried his head's impression and a couple of his silvery stray hairs—and whispered, "I love you, Thomas. I miss you, and I forgive you."

Looking back, her words seemed to foreshadow the journey we had involuntarily begun: a journey on which our dad's choice had enlisted us, a journey of discovering the power of forgiveness and unconditional love that lay within me.

As I mourned the loss of my dad, I simultaneously welcomed the life of my second newborn daughter and watched as my husband embarked on a battle with drug addiction that would later take our marriage and nearly his life. Just when I needed him the most, my husband emotionally left our marriage. His choices tutored me further about this precious gift of agency as I saw firsthand the devastating ripple effect of the painful consequences.

Mack's addiction to drugs taught me how to depend on God. I felt much like the brother of Jared who, for every thing he needed, cried unto the Lord: "And behold, O Lord, in them there is no light; whither shall we steer? And also we shall perish, for in them we cannot breathe, save it is the air which is in them; therefore we shall perish" (Ether 2:19). I remember brushing my teeth one night in the middle of Mack's addiction, thinking, "Hurry, Sophia, in just a minute you will be praying, and you will know what to do." I remember my cries unto the Lord, "What will I do? How will I provide for my kids? What if Mack dies? How should I sell this car? What about my Eternal Family? Am I going to be alone forever?" And on and on. I learned how to ask, and I learned that I would always receive.

> For behold, ye shall be as a whale in the midst of the sea; for the mountain waves shall dash upon you. Nevertheless, I will bring you up again out of the depths of the sea; for the winds have gone forth from out of my mouth, and also the rains and the floods have I sent forth. (Ether 2:24)

Mack and I met while serving in the England Leeds Mission. We didn't "like" each other on our missions, but we respected each other. He was my A.P. Four months after our missions, Mack asked me out. Not long after that we fell in love and married. About four years into our marriage, Mack had a jaw injury for which his doctor put him on painkillers for about three months while we waited for our insurance to pay for his surgery. In that short time, he became addicted to prescription drugs.

This was when things became very difficult in our home. Mack was terribly moody. He was gone all the time. I spent countless days and nights driving around trying to catch him at whatever he was up to. He lied compulsively, and I caught him in most of his lies. A book I read, written for families of addicts, summed up exactly how I felt: "Nothing will drive a person crazier faster than being lied to." That is precisely how I felt—crazy. I was the mom of a newborn and two-year-old, still grieving the death of my father, and now watching my husband slip away with precious little I could do about it.

The ripple effects of Mack's choices were like tidal waves drowning the people who loved him the most: myself, his daughters, his parents, and both of our families. Everyone suffered.

It was like running a spiritual marathon. Each little step I took in handling Mack's addiction felt like my spirit was being conditioned. This was not a pretty time. The reality of it was that it was brutal for all involved. A few things kept me afloat: my daughters, my family (especially my angel mom), the temple, and prayer.

One night as I went to bed I recall praying and saying to Heavenly Father, "Can't he just die? Really—wouldn't that be the best? The odds are so against him on any chance of recovery. Why should my girls have to live their lives wondering where their dad is or if he is clean?" That night, I had a vivid dream of Mack standing at the end of an airport terminal and our two girls running toward him with backpacks bouncing on their backs. He lifted them up and twirled them around. Then I heard, "Who are you to decide the worth of this soul? Who are you to say he can't recover?"

Such answers to prayers came in my dreams and in my heart; and they always came. The answer finally came to divorce Mack, but I was to wait until June. I had been told many times by my attorneys and other professionals, "Mack is not going to change. Let's just get this over with." And yet, I could not disobey what I knew I had been told. The more I learned about his disease of dependency, the easier my choice became. I discovered a love deep inside me, a love that said, "I love you enough to let go and let you learn from your choices." The Spirit told me over and over again that it would take Mack losing everything in order to change.

In the meantime, Mack went in and out of rehabs, continued using drugs, and finally left the state. I sent him divorce papers. Mack was very upset. He said he was clean. He was sorry. He wanted to do all he could to make up for what he had done. He didn't contest one thing. But it was also in these months that I was learning.

I discovered things about myself that I didn't like and a few things I did. I uncovered a part of me deep down that was like an unstoppable freight train. I named this part of my personality, "Magenta." She was ferocious and relentless but proved to be invaluable in keeping me going through the worst times—times when all I could eat was Mrs. Cavanaugh's Penuche fudge and Diet Coke, and times when I felt like I had been robbed of everything I lived for because of someone else's agency.

The turning point came when I remembered that I still had choices. I remember saying to Mack, "You can do drugs the rest of your life. You can live on the street and even kill yourself. But you will never decide how I am going to think and feel. I will always choose to love you and teach your children to love you, as well." Then I did the unfathomable and thanked him for what he had put me through, because in the end his addiction taught me precious lessons that were necessary for me to grow. I humbled myself and asked for his forgiveness for any part I played in the pain he had suffered.

Another turning point came when I was at my lowest, having almost given up hope that Mack would ever recover. I missed my dad and wanted his advice. I prayed and pleaded with Heavenly Father to let me feel my dad. Before his death, our family had received an assurance that my dad would be able to do more from beyond the veil than he would on earth. I had had dreams about my dad and had heard him whisper to me, but I hadn't felt him for a long time. I wondered why Heavenly Father wouldn't let me have my dad near me, especially now as I needed him most. I continued to pray, but with anger and annoyance, I declared, "I think You are rude. I think it is mean to leave me here on my bedroom floor wondering how I am going to get up in the morning, and You won't even let me feel my dad near me!" And then I heard ever so clearly a voice say, "I am your Father, and you will rely on me." I now knew where my dependency would be. In that agonizing moment in my suburb of Gethsemane, I knew I was being taught the intricate dynamics of agency and dependency. It was then that my bond and relationship with my Father in Heaven, my source of Love and Hope, was realized without doubt. What a gift. In that moment of anxiety, anger and insecurity, I found my ultimate freedom. Victor Frankl said, "Everything can be taken from a man but one thing: the last of the human freedoms—to choose one's attitude in any given set of circumstances, to choose one's own way" (p. 86). I had a choice.

You may be familiar with the strategy by which monkeys are often tragically caught. It has been discovered that placing peanuts in a hole within the trunk of a tree will attract monkeys. Following the smell, they climb the tree, push their small hands through the hole and grab the peanuts. The hole is just big enough for their hands to slide in; however, when clutching peanuts inside the hole, their fists cannot come out. You would think the monkeys would simply let go of the peanuts to free themselves from the tree, but they do not, even in extreme danger.

Many of us clutch tightly to our fistful of peanuts, refusing to let go—even if it keeps us trapped or endangered. Even if, like the monkey, there is a banquet table prepared for us just beyond the reach of our free hands. The table is abundant with food sweet and nourishing, but few of us let go of our peanuts to feast. Those who feast at this table will never go hungry, for when the food is eaten it will automatically replenish itself: "And Jesus said unto them, I am the bread of life; he that cometh to me shall never hunger; and he that believeth in me shall never thirst. Come unto me and partake of the fruit of the tree of life; yea, ye shall eat and drink of the bread and the waters of life freely" (John 6:35; cf. Alma 5:34).

I have eaten at this table and partaken of the feast it offers. It was as simple as choosing to let go. I let go of the peanuts I had squeezed so tightly that they were rotting in my hand. My need to be right was one peanut I knew I had to let go of. Others were being judgmental, self-righteous, and holding on to my anger. Once I became accountable for how I was cultivating sadness in my life, I was empowered. In that very moment of honest inventory, I realized that if I could create sadness I could create happiness. I was not a victim, anymore.

So I let go of the peanuts that held me down. I remembered after my dad's death my mom said, "We are not going to lay down in the dirt and die. Thomas had a choice, and I have a choice. I am going to move forward with vision." This is forgiveness: letting go and moving forward with vision—letting go of the pain, the injustices, and the wrongdoings that happen to us. Forgiveness is as simple as choosing to forgive.

Healing did not come overnight. Mack and I were separated for a year and divorced for another. Learning how to forgive was a process for me. Many times it felt like a beating. But once I felt the sweet reward of this principle it became easier.

Jesus invites, "Come unto me, all ye who are heavy laden and I will give thee rest. Take my yoke upon you, and learn of me; for I am meek and lowly of heart: and ye shall find rest unto your souls. For my yoke is easy and my burden is light" (Matthew 11:28–30). Our pain and heartache are not always taken away, but they do not have to be heavy. Christ did not come to learn our lessons for us; however, he did come to lighten our loads. He came to make the way easier, to hew down the path in order to make our journey smoother.

Letting go allowed me to partake at the Lord's banquet table where I have feasted with my daughters and my husband. I have tasted the sweetness of God's healing love. I have tasted joy and have drunk from pure water: "But whosoever drinketh of the water that I shall give him shall never thirst; but the water that I shall give him shall be in him a well of water springing up into everlasting life" (John 4:14).

When Mack was so sick and I was left cleaning up the enormous mess, I received a blessing from my bishop in which I was told, "Your Father in Heaven is allowing you to experience so much pain so that he can bless you with the equal and opposite amount of joy. You will have an eternal companion who has experienced similar pain, and you will succor one another." My head could not believe it, but my heart knew it had to be Mack. And it was. Mack and I have since remarried. I can say now that my cup runneth over with joy: "And oh, what joy, and what marvelous light I did behold; yea my soul was filled with joy as exceeding as was my pain!" (Alma 36:20).

We have succored one another, and we have beat the odds. Armed with the spirit of our Savior Jesus Christ, we can let go. And in the very moment we do, our Savior fills our empty hands with "everlasting light . . . unto everlasting salvation and [we] are encircled about with the matchless beauty of His love . . . being instruments in His hand doing great and marvelous work" (Alma 26:15).

I am careful with how I talk about Mack's addiction. To me, Mack is not a drug addict or, even now, a recovered addict. He is a son of God who abused drugs. Drug abuse is part of his history, behaviors, and choices, but it is not who he is. Having said that, Mack and I both know that our story is meant to be told, and not the sugar-coated version.

Mack wants people to understand that his addiction began with prescription drugs, which led to using illegal drugs, that went on over the course of four years. In his words, "They need to know that this is in our backyard. It is a plague that is seeping through the gutters of our society and oozing into our homes. They need to know that this happens and that they are not 'bad' people if it's happening in their family!"

We were blessed with a second chance, and for that I am eternally grateful. For me, forgiveness was the key to opening the gate to rebuilding our family. It could never have happened otherwise. And while forgiveness does not promise the same happy ending for every family, the promise of peace to every mind and healing to every heart is the same.

32

Angels on the Doorstep

I left my parents home and married at age twenty-one. I divorced ten years later. No children, very simple, signed the papers and it was over. I met someone new, and I felt free. This was something I had never felt before.

It was a whirlwind romance, very passionate and very dangerous. I was hooked. No way was I going to listen to anyone's warnings. But things got violent. I had to hide the bruises with make-up and dark sunglasses to go to work. He was drinking heavily and doing drugs. The violence escalated, and he abused me in front of our two babies. That was the last straw. This time when he hit me, I saw the reaction on my little son's face; I could see his tears, and I could hear his horror. Something in me snapped, and it was like I woke up.

The details of my long-lasting court battles are painful to recount in detail. After months of harassment, in which I was forced to file a restraining order, we moved to a new city and new home. My babies were happy, and we were on our way to a new, peaceful life.

One day, my little girl asked me, "Mamita, can I talk to you in the bathroom?" I thought the request a little strange, but I went with her into my bathroom. She said she had a secret, and proceeded to tell me what happened to her at her dad's. She said that her dad left her and my little boy with their half sister and her male cousin. He took her in a room and did inappropriate things to her. I was horrified! I tried to comfort my little girl, and was so thankful that she knew she could tell me and that I would protect her and help her. I tried to comfort her, and told her it was not her fault. We went to the doctor and filed a police report, but my children were still required by the courts to go to their dad's house, even after my son confided that his cousin had hurt him with a knife. All I could do was cry. I couldn't believe it. My heart ached for my beautiful children.

The years passed, in court or mediation every month or three months, and all my jewelry and money was gone. I couldn't afford the attorney anymore, so I took over and did it myself. Meanwhile, my ex-husband harassed me by filing criminal charges against me, over and over. The charges kept being thrown out of court as unfounded, but I had so many appearances that I started to lose my jobs. The years continued to pass this way. Again I found bruises on my children. More hospital visits. More protective services reports. More social workers, but nothing changed.

Over time, I received a call from the Supervising Inspector of the District Attorney's Office. He explained that he had a master's in Criminal Psychology and believed that my ex-husband had another personality, which he had revealed when he made death threats against me in front of the inspector. The inspector told me to file another restraining order immediately. I followed every word he said.

The judge that heard the case on this particular day was one that had helped me in the past with many child support issues. Off to court we went again. I finally heard the gavel hit its base with the words I longed to hear: "Sole custody, zero contact." We won our freedom, and my legs gave way. I had to hold onto the table in front of me. All I could say was "God bless you, your Honor." I looked back at the social worker, who had spoken on our behalf, and our dear inspector with tears in my eyes. The look on both their faces that day spoke volumes, justice had been done. When I told my two young children, they jumped up and down and said, "Mommy, now every Friday will be fun Friday!" No more nightmarish weekend exchanges.

What followed were the children's nightmares and behavioral problems due in part to the trauma they had experienced. I was at the lowest point of my life. One night, I got down on my knees and begged Heavenly Father with all of my broken heart to help me and send me angels. Suddenly, I heard the knock at the door. Standing at the door were two beautiful missionary sisters from The Church of Jesus Christ of Latter-day Saints. I invited them into our apartment, and they showed my children and me the way home. As we prayed for confirmation of the truth of the gospel of Jesus Christ, we started to heal and change our lives. After going to the temple, I received confirmation that I was home and our Heavenly Father loves us.

Even when things seemed hopeless, I never gave up on my Lord and Savior. When I called to him in my darkest hour, he sent me his angels, my dear sister missionaries, to show me the way. God was with us, and I hung onto Him with all of my hope and faith. And He saved us. There is always tomorrow, and there is always hope. Believe it with all your heart!

33

Whole

When I was twenty-five years old, my husband decided that he didn't want to be married, anymore. Our marriage had been tumultuous for several years, and the conflict only escalated when he entered medical school. With a temple marriage and three children, I was committed to him and keeping our family together; so I insisted that we go to marriage counseling.

Shortly thereafter, while in the celestial room of the Las Vegas temple, my husband informed me that because of my "pride and unwillingness to change," I was responsible for the destruction of our marriage. Then he turned on his heels and walked out of the celestial room. My eyes started gushing as waves of grief rolled over me. A temple matron asked me if I was okay. "I am so miserable," was all I could respond.

The next few years were a living nightmare. My husband and his father, both physicians, went to great lengths to attempt to prove me unfit to raise our three children, ages 1, 3, and 5. Years of legal battle ensued, dragging me through custody evaluations, therapy visits, and guardian ad litem intervention. The court eventually realized that not one of the accusations against me was true, but damage had been done. I felt betrayed, emotionally depleted, and in despair. My children had suffered the heartbreak of a broken family. My family had endured years of angst and financial expense from endless court battles. Most of our mutual friends would no longer talk to me. And I had some pretty major trust issues.

Thankfully, I never stopped trusting our Savior—and he literally carried me through the most difficult time of my life. When I couldn't find where my husband had taken our little boy, I couldn't eat and lost ten pounds in a week. Yet at the same time, I felt a constant presence of peace surround me during my darkest weeks. The companionship of the Holy Ghost literally covered my despairing soul with a blanket of peace that allowed me to keep going. I now understood what it meant to have the Holy Ghost as a comforter and a constant companion.

Though my father was away on business and wasn't able to give me a father's blessing, I was able to receive one from our stake patriarch and family friend. In the blessing, I was told that Heavenly Father was proud of me for trying so hard to keep our marriage together. He assured me that if things could work out, they would—but that I needed to remember that my husband had his agency. If my marriage fell apart, I was promised that I "would have great joy and happiness in years to come." I held onto that blessing for years and had faith that no matter how hard life was right now, Heavenly Father would give me great joy in the future.

My inspired bishop asked me to meet with a woman from LDS Family Services who had some experience working with women in my situation. When I met Susan, I knew that I could trust her. She listened to me, sympathized with me, and helped me change from a codependent, distraught girl into a confident, secure woman. Throughout our visits, she continually referred to Romans 8:28: "And we know that all things work together for good to them that love God, to them who are the called according to his purpose." Her promise to me was that if I continued to love God, then every trial—even this one—would work to my eventual advantage. I pondered that scripture every day and looked forward to its fulfillment.

With all the trials the divorce had inflicted, the most difficult was having to face the fact that I had failed. My parents had expressed reservations about my marriage in the first place, and I had to humble myself and admit that I should have listened to them. My grandma helped me get to the place where I could acknowledge that I had made a mistake; and when I finally did, I felt liberated. I was finally ready to repent. I knelt often in grief and sorrow during those years, asking Heavenly Father to forgive me for my mistakes and for neglecting to listen to the Spirit. Though I had failed on some counts, I felt the love of Heavenly Father and Jesus fill my heart—and I knew that I was forgiven. This knowledge in itself changed my life. I no longer worried about failing. As long as I depended on the Savior, I would have His love to fill my heart and His Spirit to guide me. And even if I never married again, I knew that was enough.

Eventually, my prayers of sorrow became prayers of joy. After two-and-a-half years of being a single mom, I met my wonderful husband, John. From the moment we first spoke, I knew that I could trust him. That trust blossomed into love, as he accepted me completely and loved my children without reservation. I fell in love not just with his amazing qualities, but also with his soul. His faithfulness and love for the gospel were evident from the beginning, and I felt amazed and so blessed that he would be interested in me. We have now been married for five years and have been blessed with two more children, giving us five altogether. Though our family is a blended one—complicated by joint custody, step-parenting, and weekend visits away—our children are happy and at peace. I nearly cried for joy when our son said, "Even though the divorce was hard, I would do it again to have all my sisters."

I found out what our wonderful patriarch meant when he said I would have "great joy and happiness in years to come." I am happier than I have ever been in my life, and I am so grateful to Heavenly Father for giving me a second chance. I am far from perfect, but through the Atonement of Christ, I have been made whole.

Index

A

abuse, 2, 23, 24, 25, 26, 194
addiction, 23, 24, 25, 26, 33, 47, 100, 106, 188, 189, 191, 194
anxiety, 33, 36, 94, 96, 158, 176, 191
Atonement, i, iii, xi, 2, 3, 43, 51, 52, 61, 62, 109, 123, 125, 150, 151, 160, 179,
    185, 186, 201

B

bishop, 6, 7, 9, 13, 54, 107, 168, 172, 176, 193, 200
burden, 54, 57, 109, 193
buying a home, 36

C

change, embracing, 42
children, xii, 3, 12, 16, 18, 21, 23, 25, 26, 28, 29, 30, 31, 32, 35, 39, 40, 41, 42,
    43, 45, 46, 47, 48, 49, 53, 55, 56, 57, 58, 59, 60, 63, 64, 65, 70, 71, 72,
    73, 79, 80, 82, 83, 90, 93, 94, 99, 101, 105, 107, 108, 112, 113, 114, 115,
    117, 118, 119, 121, 122, 123, 124, 127, 128, 129, 130, 132, 133, 134,
    135, 148, 149, 152, 157, 158, 159, 160, 161, 162, 163, 164, 165, 168,
    169, 170, 172, 176, 177, 178, 180, 181, 182, 183, 184, 185, 186, 191,
    195, 196, 197, 199, 200, 201

M

mercy, 6, 35, 52, 57, 61, 67, 159, 181, 182
mid-life crisis, 49, 121
miracle, 34, 37, 71, 161
Moore, Thomas, 19

N

natural man, 52

O

Oaks, Dallin H., 203

P

peace, 7, 36, 47, 67, 70, 90, 96, 108, 124, 125, 126, 135, 136, 139, 163, 182,
    183, 194, 200, 201
prayer, 5, 13, 56, 59, 60, 61, 88, 94, 96, 151, 184, 185, 190
pre-mortal experience, 17
priesthood, 14, 15, 64, 65, 78, 164, 170, 177

Q

Qualities of eternal mate, 15

R

reaping, what is sown, 64
rejection, 2, 55, 64, 65, 117, 148, 160
remarriage, 9, 16, 18, 39

S

scriptures, 14, 42, 52, 60, 61, 62, 67, 70, 71, 962, 109, 122, 159, 160, 163, 171,
    180, 182, 183, 184, 185, 200
shock, 3, 12, 37, 39, 51, 66, 105, 138, 146, 170, 181
shoelaces, analogy of, 62
single adult conference, 82, 85
singles dance, 85
singles ward, 6, 15, 18
slow and steady, 34
speed dating, 82, 83, 88
Spirit, 16, 34, 52, 107, 108, 124, 146, 151, 180, 183, 190, 201
statistics of divorce, 1

strength, 30, 31, 32, 35, 37, 42, 59, 60, 61, 62, 64, 70, 79, 80, 88, 90, 95, 124,
    135, 140, 141, 142, 148, 162, 168, 169, 183, 185
suicide, thoughts of, 12
support, of family and friends, 5, 14, 16, 23, 29, 30, 36, 57, 62, 63, 66, 68, 70,
    71, 74, 79, 95, 108, 110, 114, 117, 119, 133, 135, 139, 143, 158, 168,
    170, 196

T

temple 1, 11, 12, 14, 15, 16, 17, 18, 22, 23, 35, 36, 70, 89, 109, 132, 152, 159,
    164, 165, 190, 197, 199
testimony, 14, 15, 37, 57, 62, 71, 80
trials, 2, 6, 15, 16, 17, 19, 37, 65, 66, 90, 99, 142, 155, 159, 184, 201
tribulation, 16
trust, 34, 41, 43, 165, 172

V

vacations, 30
Valentine's Day, 49, 50, 179, 180
verbal abuse, 22
victim, 47, 99, 100, 143, 192

W

wholeness, through Atonement of Jesus Christ, 201
wisdom, 21, 35, 57, 59, 64, 135, 152, 155

Praise for *Hope After Divorce*

This collection of remarkable real life stories is profound to say the least. The insight and eternal perspective expressed by each author, speaking from personal experience, having endured incredible challenges in a marriage relationship, provides valuable messages of hope, faith, endurance and trust for those who face the challenges of life.

The reality of mortality and the capacity to endure with unwavering faith in God, with unrelenting determination to move forward is a message that can be impacting for every reader.

—Ardeth G. Kapp
General Young Women President (1984–1992)

Hope After Divorce captures powerful and remarkable testimonies of hope and faith in the Atonement of Jesus Christ by women who confronted the pain and trauma of divorce. These testimonies provide a practical Christlike road map that shows that just as there is life after death and the promise of eternal life, there is also a resurrection, a new life after divorce, and a promise of eternal happiness.

—Elder Charles A. Didier, Emeritus
First Quorum of the Seventy

President Howard W. Hunter once observed that "whatever God lays his hands upon lives." Indeed, through the Infinite Atonement of His Beloved Son, our Father in heaven extends His lifting, liberating, and healing influence to each of us, especially during distressful and disappointing seasons of our lives. The essays within Hope After Divorce are both sweet and substantive. They remind us that He who descended below all things, He who thereby knows firsthand what it feels like to be rejected or betrayed or dismissed, even He has the power to cradle us amidst any care and replace ashes with beauty, despair with hope, pain with perspective and peace. This is an important book. I highly recommend it!

—Robert L. Millet, Ph.D.
Abraham O. Smoot Professor
Emeritus Dean, Religious Education, BYU

A wonderful compilation of true life experiences of the plague of our time—divorce. It will assist all to go from not just surviving but to thriving. This book certainly offers a brightness of hope to those who find themselves in the dark and lonely hallways of divorce.

The Atonement of Jesus Christ not only offers renewal through repentance for sin, but also healing for all pain, sorrow, anguish and affliction.

—Elder Duane B. Gerrard
Second Quorum of the Seventy (1997–2003)

About the Editors

Jennifer Cummings received her Ph.D. from the University of Utah, where she has taught in the Department of Communication for almost a decade. Her research interests include interpersonal communication and family relationships. A passionate teacher, she is the recipient of the Ramona W. Cannon Teaching Award and the International Communication Association Graduate Teaching Award. She also enjoys working as a communication consultant and mediator. Her greatest joy is being a mom to her busy and beautiful daughter.

Lisa LaBelle is the founder and director of business and program development for OnBoard Outfitters, LLC. She earned her B.S. degree in Education from the University of Utah and has been teaching in academic and fitness settings for over 25 years. Lisa is a family and child advocate. Her most important work has been raising her two wonderful sons.

Amy Osmond Cook is a faculty associate at Arizona State University and teaches communication, technical writing, and interdisciplinary courses. Her publications include books such as *Full Bloom: Cultivating Success* (2011) and *Why They Believe* (2011). She received her M.A. in English from Brigham Young University and Ph.D. in Communication from the University of Utah. Amy and her husband, Jeff, are the proud parents of five children.

CPSIA information can be obtained at www.ICGtesting.com
Printed in the USA
267235BV00004B/3/P